MAXnotes®

George Orwell's

1984

Text by
Karen Brodeur
(M.A.T., Bridgewater State College)
Chairperson, Department of English
Fairhaven High School
Fairhaven, Massachusetts

Illustrations by
Karen Pica

Cirencester College, GL7 1XA
Telephone: 01285 640994

REA *Research & Education Association*

MAXnotes® for 1984

Printed in the United States of America

Library of Congress Control Number 2001116977

International Standard Book Number 0-87891-996-1

MAXnotes® is a registered trademark of
Research & Education Association, Piscataway, New Jersey 08854

What **MAXnotes®** Will Do for You

This book is intended to help you absorb the essential contents and features of George Orwell's *1984* and to help you gain a thorough understanding of the work. Our book has been designed to do this more quickly and effectively than any other study guide.

For best results, this **MAXnotes** book should be used as a companion to the actual work, not instead of it. The interaction between the two will greatly benefit you.

To help you in your studies, this book presents the most up-to-date interpretations of every section of the actual work, followed by questions and fully explained answers that will enable you to analyze the material critically. The questions also will help you to test your understanding of the work and will prepare you for discussions and exams.

Meaningful illustrations are included to further enhance your understanding and enjoyment of the literary work. The illustrations are designed to place you into the mood and spirit of the work's settings.

The **MAXnotes** also include summaries, character lists, explanations of plot, and section-by-section analyses. A biography of the author and discussion of the work's historical context will help you put this literary piece into the proper framework of what is taking place.

The use of this study guide will save you the hours of preparation time that would ordinarily be required to arrive at a complete grasp of this work of literature. You will be well prepared for classroom discussions, homework, and exams. The guidelines that are included for writing papers and reports on various topics will prepare you for any added work which may be assigned.

The **MAXnotes** will take your grades "to the max."

Dr. Max Fogiel
Program Director

Contents

> **Each chapter includes List of Characters, Summary, Analysis, Study Questions and Answers, and Suggested Essay Topics.**

MAXnotes® are simply the best – but don't just take our word for it...

"... I have told every bookstore in the area to carry your MAXnotes. They are the only notes I recommend to my students. There is no comparison between MAXnotes and all other notes ..."
  – High School Teacher & Reading Specialist,
  Arlington High School, Arlington, MA

"... The two MAXnotes titles that I have used have been very, very useful in helping me understand the subject matter reviewed. Thank you for creating the MAXnotes series ..."
  – Student, Morrisville, PA

A Glance at Some of the Characters

Winston Smith

Big Brother

O'Brien

Julia

Ampleforth

Winston's Mother & Sister

Jones, Aaronson & Rutherford

Martin

SECTION ONE

Introduction

The Life and Work of George Orwell

George Orwell (the pen name of Eric Arthur Blair) was a distinguished British journalist, essayist, pamphleteer, and novelist distinguished for his writings about the social and political issues of his time. He was born on June 25, 1903, in Bengal, where his father was a civil servant with the British colonial administration in India and Burma. Later he attended schools in England, including Eton.

From 1922-1927 Orwell served with the Indian Imperial Police in Burma, where his experiences intensified his hatred of Imperialism. Orwell wrote *Burmese Days*, published in New York in 1934, following his resignation from the force.

Orwell lived in Paris and London from 1928-1934, where he worked a series of low-paying jobs while writing numerous articles and translations. He described the poverty of these days in *Down and Out in Paris and London* (1933), his first work published under the pseudonym "George Orwell," the name inspired by the Orwell River.

Orwell wrote several novels from 1935-1939. These were: *A Clergyman's Daughter* (1935), *Keep the Aspidistra Flying* (1936), and *The Road to Wigan Pier* (1937).

In 1936 Orwell joined the anti-Fascists in Barcelona. He was wounded in the throat after fighting for a short time in the Spanish Civil War. He returned to England and wrote *Homage to Catalonia* (1938), which reflected his disillusionment with communism, and *Coming Up For Air* (1939), which, like *1984*, foreshadowed a society headed for destruction.

By that time (1940-1945) Orwell had come to view himself primarily as a political writer. He became literary editor of the *Labour Weekly Tribune*, and he frequently contributed to *The Observer*. His articles were well-received. During World War II Orwell wrote and broadcast for the British Broadcasting Company (BBC).

Orwell's later works reflected his increasing disillusionment with Russian communism. He published the essays: *Inside the Whale* (1944), *Critical Essays* (1946), and *Shooting an Elephant* (1950).

By far, however, Orwell's most popular works are the political satires *Animal Farm* (1945) and *1984* (1949). The fable *Animal Farm* attacks Revolutionary and post-Revolutionary Russia. *1984*, written during Orwell's final illness, warns of the dangers of life in a totalitarian state.

In 1949, Orwell received the *Partisan Review* award for distinguished writing, with a citation for "singular directness and honesty, a scrupulous fidelity to his experience that has placed him in that valuable clan of the writer who is a witness to his time."

After a long period of declining health, Orwell died from tuberculosis on January 21, 1950.

Historical Background

1984 is George Orwell's most famous and enduring work, with the possible exception of his political fable *Animal Farm*. The novel has been translated into more than 60 languages, condensed in the *Reader's Digest*, made into two movies, and presented on television.

The widespread impact of *1984* is evidenced by the changes in language that it effected. Today, the word "Orwellian" refers to any regimented and dehumanized society. Words like "Newspeak," "unperson," "doublethink," and "thoughtcrime" have become part of the English language. And the familiar phrase "Big Brother Is Watching You" has become synonymous with the concept of a totalitarian state.

1984's influence on other twentieth-century works has been considerable: Ray Bradbury's *Fahrenheit 451* (1954) shares the theme of repression and the destruction of a culture (in this case, books), and Anthony Burgess's *A Clockwork Orange* (1962) shares a British setting as well as an invented language, much like the Newspeak of Oceania.

Orwell thought of writing *1984* as early as 1940, during World War II, but he did not complete it until 1948 when the Cold War was beginning. The anti-Fascist writing of the 1930s and 1940s had a profound influence on Orwell, and is reflected in his writing. Moreover, events in Communist Russia also impacted the plot and theme of *1984*. From 1922 when Lenin suffered a stroke until 1928—four years after his death—there was a power struggle between Leon Trotsky, Minister of War, and Joseph Stalin, then Secretary of the Communist party. Stalin continued to grow even more influential as a member of the Politbureau, a small group of party bosses where his function was to manage the day-to-day activities of the Communist party. In 1921 Stalin became liaison between the Central Control Commission and the Central Committee; in this capacity he could control the purges designed to keep the party pure. He used this position to his advantage.

Stalin, along with allies Zinoviev and Kamenev, soon proved invincible as they utilized the secret police to put down all plots against them. While resisting Trotsky's urges to somewhat democratize the party, they eliminated his followers by sending them abroad. Trotsky was forced to resign as Minister of War. He was later expelled from the Politbureau, exiled from Russia, and eventually assassinated by one of Stalin's secret police.

From 1928 until World War II, Stalin enjoyed supreme power in Russia. Among the changes he brought to Russian life were collective agriculture, industrialization with forced labor, and the build-up of the authoritarian state combined with the annihilation of all political opposition. In 1928 began the era of the Five-Year Plans, each of which set ambitious goals for the next five years. The goals of the first Five-Year Plan were never actualized; nevertheless, the government announced that they had been realized in 1932. Immediately, another Five-Year Plan went into effect.

Changes were felt in Russian society as well. Freedom to choose one's job was non-existent; those who resisted were sent to labor camps. Stalin's dictatorship was complete when the vast majority of unskilled workers became controlled by a minority of loyal skilled workers and bureaucrats who enjoyed certain privileges restricted from the masses. Thus, the gulf between the classes widened and a new elite was created.

To refute contradictory information, Stalin had histories re-written to show that Lenin had favored his accession to power. He enjoyed a certain amount of hero-worship as cities were named in his honor.

There were critics, however, whom Stalin eliminated during the Great Purges of 1934-1938, which destroyed all possibility of future conspiracies. By 1936, when Stalin proclaimed the consti-tution of the Union of Soviet Socialist Republics (USSR) "the most democratic in the world," this was hardly an accurate description.

Under Stalin's dictatorship, the USSR had become a one-party state where elections were a mockery. Although all were eligible to belong to the Communist party, membership was, in fact, a privi-lege. The party was built upon a pyramidical structure with power and privilege for an elite few. At each level of the pyramid existed organizations to generate propaganda, train military personnel, and educate bureaucrats. All of these activities were designed to increase party loyalty and strength. Stalin remained a dictator through World War II until his death in 1953. Some elements in the plot of *1984* parallel this history.

Five books, in particular, seem to have had a direct impact on the creation of *1984*. Fyodor Zamyatin's *We* (1923), reviewed by Orwell in 1946, provided the idea for a futuristic, anti-Utopian frame for the novel. There are several resemblances between the works, both of which are also derived from H. G. Wells' anti-Uto-pian satire *When the Sleeper Walks* (1899). Likewise, Aldous Huxley's *Brave New World* (1932), to which *1984* is frequently compared, is set in the future and deals with a regimented society. From Arthur Koestler's *Darkness at Noon* (1941), Orwell took ideas about the at-mosphere of a totalitarian society. This "concentration camp" lit-erature details the struggle of its main character to maintain his individuality after his arrest and torture. James Burnham's *The Managerial Revolution* (1941) gave Orwell the idea for a world con-trolled by superstates. These powers became the Oceania, Eurasia, and Eastasia of *1984*.

The novel's bleak ending prompted readers and critics to take it as an attack on socialism in general and Communist Russia in particular and a prophesy of what would happen in the West should communism spread. Orwell was asked if his book should be interpreted as prophesy. He answered this question in a letter of June 1949:

> I do not believe that the kind of society I describe necessarily WILL, but I believe (allowing of course for the fact that the book is a satire) that something resembling it COULD arrive. I believe also that totalitarian ideas have taken root in the minds of intellectuals everywhere, and I have tried to draw these ideas out to their logical consequences.[1]

In 1949, some readers were also concerned that Orwell had set the novel in Britain. Orwell replied, "The scene of the book is laid in Britain in order to emphasize that the English-speaking races are not innately better than anyone else and that totalitarianism, if not FOUGHT against, could triumph anywhere."[2]

Opinions among critics have not been entirely favorable. Some point to the novel's overwhelming pessimism and its denouement as flawed, claiming the novel obviously is a reflection of Orwell's last illness. Others believe that it should be judged as a period piece bearing little relevance to today's world. After all, there was no special significance to the title. Orwell simply transposed the last two numbers of the year in which he finished the book.

Thus, it can be seen that a number of factors influenced the creation of *1984*, including literary sources and historical events. In order to understand the full impact of this novel, the student needs to be familiar with these influences.

Master List of Characters

Winston Smith–*main character of the novel, 39 years old, employee at the Ministry of Truth, inquisitive, intelligent*

Big Brother–*supreme leader of the Party, controlling force of Oceania, never physically appears in the novel but is everpresent*

---

1 J. R. Hammond, *A George Orwell Companion—A Guide to the Novels, Documents, and Essays* (New York: St. Martin's Press, 1982), pg. 172.
2 Ibid, pg. 173.

Thought Police–*secret militia; Big Brother's agents who eliminated potential rebels*

O'Brien–*member of the Inner Party, employee at the Ministry of Truth, Winston's chief*

Julia–*Winston's lover, 26-year-old employee at the Ministry of Truth, worker for the Junior Anti-Sex League*

Syme–*Winston's friend, specialist in Newspeak, employee in the Records Department*

Mr. Charrington–*63-year-old shopkeeper, rents hideaway to Winston, secret member of the Thought Police*

Ampleforth–*a poet*

Tillotson–*employee in the Records Department, disliked by Winston*

Tom Parsons–*Winston's neighbor at Victory Mansions, devoted to the Party, arrested for "thoughtcrime"*

Mrs. Parsons–*Tom's wife, about 30, looks older, possibly will be denounced by her children to the Thought Police*

Martin–*O'Brien's servant, fellow Party member*

Emmanuel Goldstein–*Enemy of the People, commander of the Brotherhood, former member of the Party, author of the "book," probably a creation of the Party*

Katharine–*Winston's wife, disappeared 11 years ago, loyal member of the Party*

Winston's mother–*disappeared years ago; appears only in Winston's dreams and vague memories*

Summary of the Novel

The concepts of free enterprise and individual freedom no longer exist in 1984. Only three superpowers remain to dominate a world of hatred, isolation, and fear. Eurasia and Eastasia are two of these superpowers. Oceania, the other, is always at war with one of them.

Winston Smith is a 39-year-old employee at the Ministry of Truth, London, located in Oceania. His world is shaped by the Party and its dictator/leader Big Brother, whose face is everywhere on posters captioned "Big Brother Is Watching You." Big Brother controls life in Oceania through the four ministries of Peace, Love, Plenty, and Truth. Winston's job at the Ministry of Truth involves revisions of historical documents and rewrites of news stories to reflect the Party's infallibility.

The Party, which carries out government policies in Oceania, rations food, issues clothing, and selects social activities. Both chocolate and tobacco are in short supply during this latest war. Winston's clothing, including his tattered pajamas, is government issued, and his evenings are spent in government-sponsored meetings.

War and hatred dominate Oceania, where the Party monitors every move and expression with telescreens, hidden microphones, and spies. The Thought Police, Big Brother's secret militia, help the Party quell any sign of revolt by eliminating all who think or behave in a disloyal fashion. Hate Week intensifies feeling against Emmanuel Goldstein, Enemy of the People, while increasing devotion to Big Brother. The Party also preaches that the proles, the majority, are natural inferiors to be kept in check.

The Party, however, does not completely control Winston. He secretly buys an illegal diary in which he writes the heresy "Down With Big Brother." In doing so, he commits the worst offense, "thoughtcrime," a Newspeak term for the "essential crime that contained all others in itself." Many of Winston's thoughts revolve around his attempts to remember various events and people from his childhood, especially his mother who had disappeared years before. Winston tries to investigate the specifics of life in London before the Revolution, but it seems the Party has been successful in eradicating all remnants of daily life in the past.

Winston enters into an affair with the free-spirited Julia, a fellow employee at the Ministry of Truth. At the beginning they view their desire for one another as a political act against the Party dominated by hate and suspicion. Since promiscuity among Party members has been forbidden, they view their affair as an act of rebellion. As the affair continues, Winston's feelings for Julia change. Although the couple knows the affair is doomed, they continue to meet secretly in an attic room above a junk shop owned by Mr. Charrington, the man who sold the diary, and later, a coral paperweight, to Winston. The lovers discuss the repressiveness of their lives and the possibility of joining the Brotherhood, the secret underground of Emmanuel Goldstein whose express purpose is to overthrow Big Brother.

At work at the Ministry of Truth, Winston is approached by O'Brien, an acquaintance who seems to share his views. After Winston and Julia visit O'Brien at his apartment, he recruits them as members of the Brotherhood and promises to send them a copy of Goldstein's book, which details strategies to destroy Big Brother. Winston pledges to do whatever it takes, including murder and suicide, to erode the power of the Party.

The inevitable occurs when Julia and Winston are arrested in their secret room, betrayed by Mr. Charrington, a member of the Thought Police. Winston is taken to the Ministry of Love where he is starved, beaten, and tortured during the next months in an effort to "cure" him. Ironically, his torturer is O'Brien, who confirms his identity as a dedicated Inner Party member. Winston submits after a long struggle when he is taken to the mysterious room 101 and threatened with a cage of hungry rats prepared to devour him. At this point he finally betrays Julia.

Soon Winston is released, but he awaits the bullet he knows will extinguish him. He unexpectedly runs into Julia, who admits that she too had betrayed their love. Surprisingly, Winston feels no desire for her, preferring instead to take his usual seat at the Chestnut Street Cafe where he spends another night in his habitual alcoholic stupor. Winston knows that it is only a matter of time before the Party executes him; nevertheless, when the telescreen barks the news of the army's latest victory, he weeps with joy. The Party finally controls Winston, whose defeat is summed up in the final sentence, "He loved Big Brother."

Estimated Reading Time

1984 is divided into three major sections of approximately equal length, each with separate chapters. Orwell also included an appendix on Newspeak. Thus, in order to maximize understanding, the reader should plan no fewer than four reading sessions.

By reading approximately 30 pages per hour, the reader should be able to complete the entire novel in 8 to 12 hours. He or she should also plan to spend more time on Part I, where Orwell establishes the frameworks of plot, characterization, and theme.

SECTION TWO

Part I

Part I, Chapter 1

New Characters:

Winston Smith: *main character, employee at the Ministry of Truth*

Big Brother: *leader/dictator of the Party*

O'Brien: *official of the Inner Party, Winston's co-worker at the Ministry of Truth*

Emmanuel Goldstein: *Enemy of the People*

Julia: *26-year-old employee at the Ministry of Truth, worker for the Junior Anti-Sex League*

Summary

On a cold afternoon in April 1984, Winston Smith returns to his apartment at Victory Mansions. He barely notices the many posters of a 45-year-old man with a black moustache whose captions read "Big Brother Is Watching You."

Inside the apartment is a telescreen through which the Thought Police monitor one's every action and sound. Winston turns his back to the telescreen and looks out on London, chief city of Airstrip One, the third most populous province of Oceania. He sees bombed sites contrasted against the gleaming Ministry of Truth, which dominates the landscape. He reads the three slogans of the party:

WAR IS PEACE
FREEDOM IS SLAVERY
IGNORANCE IS STRENGTH

Winston also sees the three other ministries of government: Peace, Love, and Plenty. The stark, windowless Ministry of Love frightens Winston because no one enters except on official business. Winston positions himself out of the telescreen's range, drinks a cup of gin, and begins a diary. If he is found out, he will probably be put to death even though laws no longer exist in Oceania. Feeling helpless, he tentatively begins "April 4, 1984"; he's not even sure of the date or of his reasons for writing the diary.

Winston remembers that an incident at work involving the Two Minutes Hate has provoked him to begin this journal. At the scene was a girl from the Fiction Department and O'Brien, a member of the Inner Party who appeared quite important. The purpose of the ritual was to increase antagonism toward Emmanuel Goldstein, Enemy of the People.

About 30 seconds into the Hate when Goldstein's face appeared on the telescreen, people reacted violently with everyone joining in. Winston, too, felt hate, but it had been directed toward the Party, Big Brother, and the Thought Police. This hate was fleeting, though, for at the next moment he adored Big Brother.

The Hate had ended with the image of Big Brother and the Party's three slogans flashing on the screen. In response, Winston's co-workers chanted their love of Big Brother. Looking at O'Brien, Winston believed that his acquaintance knew and understood his disloyal thoughts.

Remembering this incident, Winston continues his diary and absent-mindedly prints "Down With Big Brother" repeatedly. By expressing himself in this manner, he has now committed "thoughtcrime," an all-inclusive offensive whose punishment is extermination.

Analysis

The opening paragraphs of *1984* define the setting. Orwell's choice of "cold" and "vile" as well as phrases such as "swirl of gritty dust" to describe the April afternoon establish the atmosphere for

the "coldness" of the plot to follow. The appeal to the senses is especially effective. Additionally, the clock is striking "thirteen." This seemingly minor detail suggests an abnormality in the setting, which foreshadows the events that will occur there.

Orwell paints a scene of destruction as he describes wartime London. The city has been virtually destroyed with "bombed sites where plaster dust swirled in the air." Bombs have cleared paths where there have "sprung up sordid colonies of wooden dwellings like chicken houses." Some critics have compared Orwell's description of the city's bleakness to the vivid pictures of London presented in the novels of Charles Dickens. In contrast, the dominating Ministry of Truth is an enormous pyramid of "glittering white concrete" that stands out, as do the three other ministries which "dwarf the surrounding architecture."

These sights serve as the backdrop for the introduction of the protagonist Winston Smith, who observes these sights from his apartment window at Victory Mansions. Orwell's working title for this novel, *The Last Man in Europe*, suggests that his hero, an isolated, lonely figure, is the last believer in the values of the past, described in the book as pre-Revolutionary time. The surname "Smith," the most common in England, suggests the representative quality of the hero.

Winston's life, like the landscape, is dominated by the four ministries: Truth, Peace, Love, and Plenty, which are "led" by the dictator Big Brother, who, most critics believe, represents Russia's supreme dictator, Stalin. In fact, this control by the Party is the basis for the central conflict: restrictions of the totalitarian state under which Winston lives versus his growing restlessness with the rigidity of his life and his concern that the past as a shaper of history will be erased or forgotten.

Although Winston is only a member of the Outer Party, he is extremely intelligent. Scholars believe that this quality is Winston's downfall. Orwell describes Winston's unfocused hatred as he sits with his coworkers during the Two Minutes Hate:

> Thus, at one moment Winston's hatred was
> not turned against Goldstein at all, but, on the
> contrary, against Big Brother, the Party, and the

Thought Police; and at such moments his heart went out to the lonely, derided heretic on the screen, sole guardian of truth and sanity in a world of lies. And yet the very next instant he was at one with the people about him, and all that was said of Goldstein seemed to him to be true. At those moments his secret loathing of Big Brother changed into adoration....

Despite having the outward appearance of a loyal, controlled Party member, Winston is capable of independent thoughts. Orwell continues:

Winston succeeded in transferring his hatred from the face on the screen to the dark-haired girl behind him. Vivid, beautiful hallucinations flashed through his mind....He would ravish her and cut her throat at the moment of climax. Better than before, moreover, he realized *why* it was that he hated her.

Knowing that the consequences of his action will be death, Winston begins a secret diary. The writing is therapeutic, although crude, and the diary allows him to express several forbidden thoughts including the death sentence, "Down With Big Brother." Thus, the opening chapter of this novel clearly points toward the logical consequences of the events in the plot.

Study Questions

1. When does the novel begin?
2. Where does the novel begin?
3. Cite the caption on the posters in Winston's building.
4. What is Newspeak?
5. What does a telescreen do?
6. What are the Party's three slogans?
7. Name the four Ministries of the government.
8. What is the purpose of the Two Minutes Hate?

9. What is thoughtcrime?

10. What is the penalty for thoughtcrime?

Answers

1. The novel begins at 13 o'clock on a day in April 1984.

2. The novel begins at Victory Gardens.

3. The caption on the posters reads "Big Brother Is Watching You."

4. Newspeak is the official language of Oceania.

5. A telescreen monitors one's every motion and sound.

6. The Party's three slogans are: War Is Peace, Freedom Is Slavery, and Ignorance Is Strength.

7. The four Ministries are Truth, Peace, Love, and Plenty.

8. The purpose of the Two Minutes Hate is to increase hatred of Emmanuel Goldstein, Enemy of the People.

9. Thoughtcrime is an all-inclusive crime.

10. The penalty for thoughtcrime is extermination.

Suggested Essay Topics

1. Discuss the omnipresent posters of Big Brother in terms of his physical appearance as well as the phrase "Big Brother Is Watching You." What does the caption imply about the society in which Winston Smith lives? Are these implications supported by evidence from Chapter 1?

2. Discuss the three party slogans and what each statement implies about this society. What does the public's easy acceptance of these mottos suggest about the populace at this stage of the story?

Part 1, Chapter 2

New Character:

Mrs. Parsons: *Winston's neighbor*

Summary

Winston's writing is interrupted by his neighbor, Comrade— or Mrs.—Parsons, who asks his help with a repair. Her children play a favorite game: Spies. Thinking of the "child heroes" who denounce their parents, Winston supposes that the Parsons' children are typical of most others. Dressed in the uniform of the Spies, the children leap about accusing Winston of all sorts of crimes, including "thoughtcrime." Mrs. Parsons explains the children's exuberance as pent-up energy because they have not been out of the house all day. It seems she has been unable to take them to the much-anticipated public execution of Eurasian soldiers, the latest prisoners of war.

Back in his apartment as he prepares to write, Winston remembers a dream in which someone whispers, "We shall meet in the place where there is no darkness." Winston believes the speaker is O'Brien, but his confusion persists as to what the message means.

The telescreen barks the announcement of another military victory followed by a long description of the execution of Eurasian soldiers. Next comes the not-so-surprising edict that the chocolate ration has been reduced. In the background Winston hears a rocket bomb explode, a constant occurrence these days.

Winston feels alone. He questions a number of factors regarding his existence. Did anyone else ever question the mutability of the past? Would the Party rule forever? Why is he writing this diary?

Winston feels there is no escape, that nothing in his life has meaning. Nevertheless, he continues his writing, expressing the idea that thoughtcrime means death. Even though Winston knows he now is marked for extermination, he hides the diary and tries to wash away the incriminating ink stains on his hands.

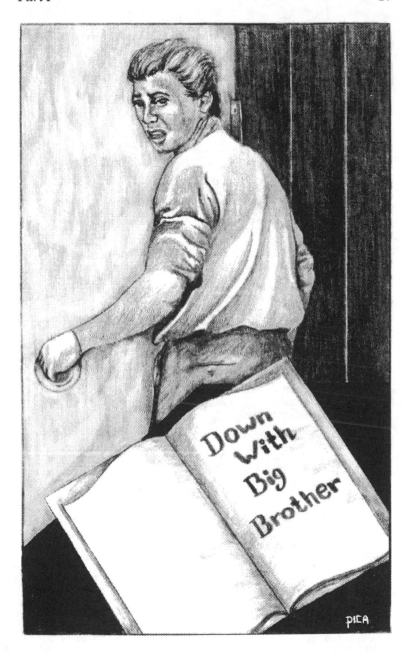

Analysis

The incident at the Parsons' apartment illustrates some everyday facets of life in Oceania. Mrs. Parsons is only 30 years old, but she looks considerably older. Her husband, occupied with Party business, is not home. Orwell depicts Mr. Parsons with little intelligence but more than enough devotion to the Party. Although we have not yet met Tom Parsons, the odor of his sweat permeates the home suggesting the hard work and drudgery that characterize his life.

Even at this early age the Parsons' children are learning that disloyalty to the Party will not be tolerated. In fact, a number of children, or "child heroes," have successfully denounced their parents to the Thought Police. The children are particularly disappointed today because they will be missing the hanging of several Eurasian war prisoners. Violence seems to be an integral part of childhood. The sight of so-called innocent children engaged in play with such violent overtones is alarming but enlightening. Allegiance to the Party rather than love for one's family is cultivated at a very early age. The breakdown of family relationships is a dominant motif in this novel.

Back at his apartment, Winston continues to think of the early incident at work and of O'Brien. He believes that in a dream he has heard O'Brien whisper, "We shall meet in the place where there is no darkness." Winston has no substantial proof that O'Brien is an ally, but his hope undoubtedly is a result of desperation for camaraderie.

Against the backdrop of war and hatred, Winston feels alone. Orwell tells us, "He felt as though he were wandering in the forests of the sea bottom, lost in a monstrous world where he himself was the monster." This metaphor heightens the differences between Winston and his "comrades" by ironically emphasizing that it is not Winston who is monstrous.

Winston feels comforted by his belief that there is one thing the Party cannot take: the thoughts inside one's skull. The struggle for Winston's thoughts will become a dominant theme. Perhaps it is this conviction that prompts Winston to continue the diary, but as Orwell explicitly states, writing it means certain death.

Study Questions

1. What form of address has replaced "Mrs."?

2. What game are the Parsons' children playing?

3. Give the crime the children accuse Winston of committing.

4. What popular spectacle took place that afternoon?

5. What is a "child hero"?

6. Who speaks in Winston's dream?

7. What does the speaker in the dream tell Winston?

8. What is the bad news delivered via the telescreen?

9. Winston addresses his diary to whom or to what?

10. Explain why Winston washes his hands before he returns to work.

Answers

1. The new form of address is "Comrade."

2. The Parsons' children are playing Spies.

3. The children accuse Winston of committing thoughtcrime.

4. A public execution was the popular spectacle that took place that afternoon.

5. A "child hero" is an eavesdropper who has denounced his parents to the Thought Police.

6. O'Brien speaks in Winston's dream.

7. The speaker in the dream tells Winston, "We shall meet in the place where there is no darkness."

8. The bad news was that the chocolate ration would be reduced from 30 grams to 20.

9. Winston addresses his diary to a time when freedom of thought is the norm.

10. Winston washes this hands because ink stains might reveal that he has been writing.

Suggested Essay Topics

1. Examine the ways in which the Party makes itself stronger by influencing the youth of Oceania. Discuss the daily lives of the Parsons' children. What are their favorite games? How do they like to dress? What seems to be their attitude toward thoughtcrime?

2. Discuss Winston's need to continue his diary despite the obvious implications of capture and punishment.

Part 1, Chapter 3

New Character:

Winston's mother: *appears only in Winston's dreams, disappeared many years ago*

Summary

Winston only vaguely remembers his parents, who disappeared in one of the Great Purges of the fifties. Winston's only memory of his father is of the thin soles on his shoes.

He recalls his mother and sister in a vivid dream where, as passengers on a sinking ship, they clutch one another right before it falls to the bottom of the sea. From the expression on his mother's face, Winston can see that she died loving him. Winston is struck by the impossibility of this emotion's existence in a society now dominated by war and hatred. Things have certainly changed since her disappearance when Winston was only 10 or 11.

His mind wandering, Winston drifts to a recurrent dream of a young girl approaching him in an open meadow that he calls the Golden Country. As she draws nearer, she throws off her clothes and gestures to Winston with a single, graceful movement of her arm. Winston is especially captivated by the freedom with which she makes this gesture.

A screaming telescreen leading the morning calisthenics awakens Winston who is muttering the word "Shakespeare." He finds these exercises particularly difficult as the exertion always leads to

a coughing fit, but Winston continues to think as he mechanically follows through with the Physical Jerks.

Reminiscing about the past, Winston does not remember a time without war, which currently is being waged against Eurasia. Only four years before, Oceania had fought Eastasia, but since no official records now exist, the war officially never happened. Winston senses that this knowledge existing in his consciousness will soon be annihilated. The Party slogan, "Who controls the past controls the future: who controls the present controls the past," is frightening to him.

Winston continues to exercise as he tries unsuccessfully to remember when he'd first heard of Big Brother. He also recalls Ingsoc—"English Socialism"—but he cannot exactly remember when the phrase was first popularized. His thoughts are interrupted, and he is brought back to reality by the irate voice on the telescreen, which is not satisfied with his morning routine.

Analysis

Orwell introduces the dream motif in this chapter. Winston's dream about his mother's and sister's disappearance serves two purposes. First, its setting on a sinking ship forecasts the hopeless future for the society in which Winston grew up. By the time Winston reaches adulthood, only remnants of family life as he knew it remain. Undoubtedly, Orwell is satirizing Stalin's Great Purges during which seven million were arrested, one-half million were executed, and 2.5 million died in labor camps.

Secondly, the dream allows Winston to explore his feelings about his mother's death, which he characterizes as tragic. Especially moving is the knowledge that although she was sacrificed for her son, Winston's mother died loving him. Orwell observes, "Such things, he saw, could not happen today. Today there were fear, hatred, and pain, but no dignity of emotion, or deep and complex sorrows."

Equally revealing is Winston's second dream. Surprisingly, it is not the girl's nakedness that fascinates Winston, but instead the utter freedom with which she gestures to him. This gesture is reminiscent of other times and individuals.

Orwell continues to develop the concept of his protagonist as an independent freethinker. Even though morning exercises are consuming all of Winston's physical energy, mentally he continues to dwell on the past. The Party's slogan, "Who controls the past controls the future: who controls the present controls the past," alarms Winston because he can see evidence that this policy is becoming reality. The war against Eastasia four years ago has been completely obliterated from records and history books; therefore, it never happened. The mutability of the past with control by the Party is a major theme in this novel.

Study Questions

1. How old was Winston when his mother disappeared?
2. What is the only thing Winston remembers about his father?
3. What does Winston surmise happened to his parents?
4. Where are Winston's mother and sister in his dream?
5. Who appears in Winston's second dream?
6. What is Winston muttering as he awakens?
7. What is Airstrip One?
8. With whom is Oceania at war?
9. What is the Party slogan?
10. What is Ingsoc?

Answers

1. Winston was 10 or 11 years old when his mother disappeared.
2. Winston only remembers the thin soles on his father's shoes.
3. Winston believes his parents were probably swallowed up in one of the purges of the fifties.
4. Winston's mother and sister are in the saloon of a sinking ship.
5. A dark-skinned girl who flings off her clothes appears in Winston's dream.

6. Winston is muttering "Shakespeare" as he awakens.

7. Airstrip One was formerly known as England.

8. Oceania is at war with Eurasia.

9. The Party slogan is: "Who controls the past controls the future: who controls the present controls the past."

10. Ingsoc is the Newspeak form of "English Socialism."

Suggested Essay Topics

1. Describe the circumstances surrounding the death of Winston's mother. What are his conflicting emotions? Tell why her death is doubly tragic, in view of societal changes since Winston's childhood.

2. Discuss the implications of Winston's dreams as acts of thoughtcrime.

Part I, Chapters 4 and 5

New Characters:

Tillotson: *employee in the Records Department*

Syme: *Winston's friend, expert in Newspeak*

Tom Parsons: *Winston's neighbor and coworker, loyal to the Party*

Summary

Winston's job at the Ministry of Truth is to alter or "rectify" records to create documentary evidence supporting the Party. As soon as he finishes with the day's assignment, he drops the instructions into the memory hole, where he assumes they are destroyed along with the papers containing the original information.

The Records Department is only a small branch of the Ministry of Truth, the primary purpose of which is to supply the citizens of Oceania with information and entertainment via newspapers, textbooks, films, novels, and telescreen programs. The Ministry also creates entirely different information on a lower level for the proles,

including the lowest form of pornography, "Pornosec," forbidden to Party members except those who have created it.

Winston loves his work, which for the most part is tedious, but in some ways challenging as he tries to anticipate what the Party wants him to say in his "revised" documents. There is a certain amount of competition among workers; Winston suspects that Tillotson, a coworker, has received the same assignment.

Today, as part of a revision of Big Brother's Order of the Day, Winston plans to commemorate the fictitious Comrade Ogilvy with a few false lines and photographs to bring this "unperson" into existence. It strikes Winston that once his work is complete, Comrade Ogilvy will exist as authentically as Charlemagne or Julius Caesar.

At work Winston sees his friend Comrade Syme, and over a dull, regulation lunch they discuss Syme's current project, the eleventh edition of the Newspeak dictionary. Syme is proud of his work streamlining the language; of particular interest is the destruction of verbs and adjectives. The new dictionary will simplify synonyms and eliminate antonyms altogether. Syme offers "ungood" as an example of how Newspeak will be able to narrow the range of thought by eliminating the finer shades of distinction within the language. Thoughtcrime will become impossible, he predicts, for there will be no words to express it.

Syme believes that by 2050 everyone will speak Newspeak except the proles, who are not considered humans. He seems especially confident that the great literature of the past, including the works of Shakespeare and Chaucer, will be destroyed. Privately, Winston believes Syme will be vaporized for his intelligence and directness. Syme's favorite hangout, the Chestnut Tree Cafe, is characterized as an "ill-omened" place where discredited leaders hang out.

The conversation is interrupted by Parsons as he collects block dues from Winston. From the telescreen comes an announcement from the Ministry of Plenty that because of the workers' superior output, the standard of living has increased at least 20 percent over the past year. Ironically, as Winston listens, he is smoking one of his few remaining cigarettes before the new rations start the next day.

Winston absorbs the announcement that there have been demonstrations honoring Big Brother for raising the chocolate ration to 20 grams a week, observing that only yesterday it had been announced that the ration was to be reduced from 30 to 20 grams. Winston wonders how people could so gullibly accept such news. Both Parsons in his stupidity and Syme with his intelligence accept it. Is Winston all alone?

Analysis

Orwell continues to explore the theme of the mutability of the past as he examines the role of the Ministry of Truth, which controls versions of information given to the Party members of Oceania and to the proles. Many literary critics believe that Orwell modeled the ministry after the BBC for which he worked during World War II. The BBC broadcasts radio and television programs to countries all over the world. Orwell's experiences at the BBC gave him insight into the dangers of government control of information.

Ironically, Winston's job at the Ministry of Truth is to falsify records for the Party, leaving no trace of the alteration itself. Orwell describes Winston at work:

> Winston's greatest pleasure in life was his work. Most of it was tedious routine, but included in it there were also jobs so difficult and intricate you could lose yourself in them as in the depths of a mathematical problem—delicate pieces of forgery in which you had nothing to guide you except your knowledge of the principles of Ingsoc and your estimate of what the Party wanted you to say.

Although Winston enjoys the process of creation itself, he continues to ponder the ethical implications of altering the past as he creates Comrade Ogilvy, a fictitious war hero. Orwell writes, "It struck him as curious that you could create dead men but not living ones. Comrade Ogilvy, who had never existed in the present, now existed in the past, and when once the act of forgery was forgotten, he would exist just as authentically, and upon the same evidence, as Charlemagne or Julius Caesar."

Orwell also begins to explore the impact of language on society through the character of Syme who is systematically destroying the language. He tells Winston, "You don't grasp the beauty of the destruction of words." When the finer shades of meaning are destroyed, Syme calls it a "...question of self-discipline, reality-control." Orwell demonstrates his belief that there is a relationship between the destruction of language and the destruction of thought. Some critics also believe that Orwell was parodying created languages in this section. Winston predicts the vaporization of Syme for his intelligence; we readers notice that same character trait in Winston. Of note also is the hangout Syme frequents, the Chestnut Tree Cafe, which Orwell terms "ill-omened," a gathering place for discredited leaders before they are purged.

Another irony in Winston's life is shown through the announcement from the Ministry of Plenty that the standard of living has risen 20 percent over the past year. Winston's reality, like the reality of Orwell's post-World War II audience, is that many goods are rationed. The government's ability to disseminate propaganda and the public's gullibility is shown here through the character of Parsons, whom Winston realizes has accepted the announcement "with the stupidity of an animal."

Study Questions

1. What is the official phrase for altering records?
2. What is the primary job of the Ministry of Truth?
3. What is "Pornosec"?
4. What is Winston's greatest pleasure in life?
5. Who is Comrade Ogilvy?
6. What is Syme's current project at the Records Department?
7. According to Syme, what is the whole aim of Newspeak?
8. What does Syme predict will have occurred by 2050?
9. Tell why Winston believes Syme will disappear one day.
10. Who does Winston believe is following him?

Answers

1. The official phrase for altering records is to "rectify" them.

2. Its primary aim is to supply information in all forms to the citizens of Oceania as well as to the proles.

3. "Pornosec" is the lowest kind of pornography, forbidden to Party members.

4. Winston's greatest pleasure in life is his work.

5. Comrade Ogilvy is a war hero who actually never existed.

6. Syme's current project is compiling the eleventh edition of the Newspeak dictionary.

7. According to Syme, the whole aim of Newspeak is to narrow the range of thought.

8. Syme's prediction is that by 2050 all knowledge of Oldspeak will have disappeared.

9. Syme will disappear one day because of his intelligence, Winston believes.

10. Winston believes that the girl from the Fiction Department is following him.

Suggested Essay Topics

1. Discuss the function of the Ministry of Truth. What is ironic about its title? Explain what Winston does there and how he feels about his work. Explain how the creation of Comrade Ogilvy supports the Party motto.

2. How would you explain both Parsons' and Syme's acceptance of obvious propaganda? Discuss the reasons.

Part I, Chapters 6 and 7

New Character:

Katharine: *Winston's wife, loyal Party member who disappeared years ago*

Summary

At home, Winston continues the illicit diary. His next entry begins with a vivid account of an encounter with a prostitute many years before. Writing this account, an exercise in frustration, makes him want to bang his head against the wall.

It occurs to Winston that one's worst enemy is his own nervous system. He thinks of a passerby on the street who was having muscle spasms; most frightening was the fact that they were unconscious. This leads Winston to observe the most deadly danger of all: talking in one's sleep.

Winston tries to refocus on the diary, but he can't. He thinks of Katharine, his wife, whom he recollects with revulsion. She truly believed what she had been taught: The only recognized purpose of marriage is to have children for the service of the Party. Finally, when the marriage had produced no children, she disappeared approximately 11 years ago.

As he finally gets his thoughts under control, Winston finishes this entry with a matter-of-fact account of a sex act with a prostitute, and then throws down the pen with disgust.

Winston explores his frustrations as he later continues to write. He believes that the only hope for the future lies with the proles who comprise 85 percent of the population. In Winston's estimation the Party could never be overthrown from within, for its enemies have no way of recognizing or meeting one another. On the other hand, the proles were the only group with enough physical force to overthrow the government should they ever become aware of their own strength.

Rebellion, however, is unlikely, for the Party controls everything, even the past. The Party claims to have liberated the proles from bondage and improved their living conditions; Winston notes that in actuality, the proles are treated like animals.

The frustration of trying to remember life before the Revolution is intensified as Winston copies into his diary a passage from a children's history book that presents life in London before the Revolution as a miserable existence.

Winston remembers the survivors of the great purges in which the original leaders of the Revolution were exterminated. Three men named Jones, Aaronson, and Rutherford were arrested, confessed to espionage and a number of other offenses, and eventually pardoned by the Party and given sinecures. Winston had seen these three at the Chestnut Tree Cafe and they were shunned—certainly doomed. Later all three were rearrested and executed as a warning to others. But five years later Winston came upon a photo through his job proving that their confessions had been lies. This would have been extremely damaging to the Party. Winston destroyed the photo by throwing it down the memory hole. The effect of this was to destroy the past, of course. Winston now knows how, but he doesn't know why.

Intuitively, Winston knows that the Party has enough power to declare that $2 + 2 = 5$, and this dictum will be accepted. The Party is powerful enough to control external reality by mind control.

Unexpectedly, Winston thinks of O'Brien and decides to write the diary for him because he believes O'Brien is on his side. Today's diary entry ends: "Freedom is the freedom to say that two plus two make four. If that is granted, all else follows."

Analysis

Writing as a means to explore feelings and vent frustrations is a central motif here as these chapters revolve around the diary. It seems logical that in these chapters, writing is a vehicle to reveal the truth, which follows and contrasts the chapters showing language as a mechanism to create lies.

Winston reveals his frustrations in the first entry exploring the Party doctrine on marriage and family life that expressly states that the only real purpose of marriage is to beget children. As Winston views the Party's doctrine, "[s]exual intercourse was to be looked on as a slightly disgusting minor operation, like having an enema." The impossibility of controlling such basic instincts is pointed out

when Winston notes that prostitution is fairly prevalent in the poorer sections of the city.

Orwell also suggests that the repression of the sexual appetite affects the body in other areas; for instance, Winston notices the unconscious twitches and spasms in a passerby. Winston himself suffers from an oozing varicose ulcer. The atmosphere of repression had invaded even the most private areas of one's life: Winston is even afraid of talking in his sleep.

Against this background lies Winston's hope for the proles. Orwell's comments about their living conditions seem directed at the Russian Revolution, which supposedly brought a better life to the masses, but, in fact, did not. His references to the great purges of the Revolution most likely are further attacks on Stalin's Great Purges. The reference to Goldstein, who fled shortly before the arrests of Jones, Aaronson, and Rutherford most likely is aimed at Leon Trotsky, who was forced into exile during Stalin's rise to power in Russia.

Winston's destruction of the photo of the three men supports the recurrent theme of the mutability of the past, but raises another question. "I understand HOW," writes Winston. "I do not understand WHY." This remains a central question of the novel.

The setting of the Chestnut Tree Cafe as a place for dissidents who eventually meet their deaths has been mentioned twice so far and hardly seems a coincidence.

Lastly, underlying all of Winston's writing is the hope that the mind is the one thing the Party cannot control; yet Winston is astute enough to know that the Party is powerful enough to declare $2 + 2 = 5$ and that the statement will be believed. The fact that the mind is a shaper of reality is a powerful message in this novel. Orwell borrowed this example from Stalin's slogan "The Five Year Plan in Four Years," which was symbolized in posters reading "$2 + 2 = 5$" placed all over Russia.

Study Questions

1. What does Winston believe is the most deadly danger of all?
2. What is the unforgivable crime?
3. What is the only recognized purpose of marriage?

4. Why did Winston call Katharine the "human soundtrack"?

5. Why does Winston believe a real love affair would be almost unthinkable?

6. What percent of Oceania's population is comprised of proles?

7. What does Winston copy into his diary?

8. What is Winston's proof that the confessions of Jones, Aaronson, and Rutherford were lies?

9. What happened to Winston's proof?

10. To whom is Winston writing the diary?

Answers

1. The most deadly danger is talking in one's sleep.

2. The unforgivable crime is promiscuity among Party members.

3. The only recognized purpose of marriage is to have children for the service of the Party.

4. Winston calls Katharine the "human soundtrack" because she repeated every Party slogan.

5. A real love affair would be almost unthinkable because chastity was an important aspect of Party loyalty.

6. Eighty-five percent of Oceania's population consists of proles.

7. Winston copies a passage from a children's history book into his diary.

8. Winston's proof is a photo of the three men in New York at a time when they supposedly had been on Eurasian soil.

9. Winston dropped his proof into the memory hole.

10. Winston is writing the diary to O'Brien.

Suggested Essay Topics

1. The Party's influence on marriage and family life has been profound. What is the Party's official position on marriage and children? To what extent was Katharine affected by this position?

2. How does the Party acknowledge that the sexual instinct may not always be controlled? Evaluate Winston's feelings about his visit to the prostitute.

Part I, Chapter 8

New Character:

Mr. Charrington: *kindly old shopkeeper*

Summary

London is bombed as the war continues. Winston, who sees a human hand in an alley, has little reaction as he kicks it into the gutter.

On this long walk he meets an old man in a bar whom he asks about life before the Revolution. The old man has no recall of anything significant; as a result, Winston's frustrations are intensified.

He wanders into the junk shop where he had bought the diary. There he buys a coral paperweight from the shopkeeper, Mr. Charrington, who seems glad for the business as antiques are not much in demand these days.

In an upstairs room Winston notices the absence of the telescreen and the presence of a print of a local church, St. Clement's Dane, now ruined because of the war. Charrington and Winston are familiar with the rhyme "Oranges and lemons, say the bells of St. Clement's," although Winston has trouble remembering the last lines. Winston feels safe and hopeful here where at least some vestiges of the past remain.

In order to avoid being detected in this area of the city, Winston soon leaves. As he exits the shop, he sees the girl from the Fiction Department. Convinced she is a spy, he hurries along.

Surely, the Thought Police will seize him, thinks Winston, who is reminded of O'Brien's statement in his dream: "We shall meet in the place where there is no darkness." At the same time he looks at a coin and is reminded:

WAR IS PEACE

FREEDOM IS SLAVERY

IGNORANCE IS STRENGTH

With these two conflicting thoughts in mind, Winston hurries home.

Analysis

Winston's growing fascination with the beauty and heritage of the past is symbolized when he buys a coral paperweight from Charrington. Orwell describes Winston's reaction:

> What appealed to him was not so much its beauty as the air it seemed to possess of belonging to an age quite different from the present one.... It was a queer thing, even a compromising thing, for a Party member to have in his possession. Anything old, and for that matter anything beautiful, was always vaguely suspect.

Orwell accomplishes much in Part I. He has established the setting and tone for the novel. His characterization of the protagonist Winston Smith is fairly complete. By now we also thoroughly understand the nature of the internal conflict that is the crux of the plot. In addition, he has introduced elements of satire and parody.

Study Questions

1. Instead of spending a night at the Community Center, where does Winston go?

2. What does the Newspeak term "ownlife" imply?

3. After the bombing, what does Winston see lying in the street?

4. What is the one public event to which the proles pay attention?

5. What does Winston learn from the old man in the bar?

6. What does Winston buy at Charrington's shop?

7. What is different about the room above Charrington's shop?

8. Why does Winston plan to return to the shop?

9. Who seems to be spying on Winston as he leaves Charrington's shop?

10. What is Winston's current interpretation of the phrase "place where there is no darkness"?

Answers

1. Winston heads into London.

2. The term implies individualism and eccentricity.

3. Winston sees a human hand lying in the street.

4. The proles pay attention to the Lottery.

5. The old man remembers nothing useful of the past.

6. Winston buys a glass paperweight with a coral center.

7. The room has no telescreen, and it has a print of St. Clement's Church.

8. Winston plans to return to buy the print, jog Charrington's memory, and, perhaps, to rent the upstairs room.

9. The girl from the Fiction Department seems to be spying on Winston.

10. Winston believes the phrase refers to the "imagined future."

Suggested Essay Topics

1. Explore Winston's attempts to hold on to the past. Tell why his conversation with the old man only increases his frustrations.

2. What does the upstairs room at Charrington's shop mean to Winston? Why does he buy the paperweight? How might this action be interpreted symbolically?

Part II

Part II, Chapter 1

Summary

Four days after spotting the girl from the Fiction Department outside the junk shop, Winston sees her at work. After falling in the corridor she is having trouble regaining her balance since her arm is in a sling. Before he tries to help, Winston feels confused. On one hand, he believes the girl might be an enemy out to kill him; on the other hand, he sees a fellow human being in need. As Winston helps her from the ground, she slips a note into his hand.

Winston returns to his work station to begin some routine task. He thinks about the note. Maybe it is a summons from the Thought Police or perhaps a message from the underground, possibly from the Brotherhood. As soon as he senses that he is not being watched, Winston opens the note which reads, "I love you." Shocked, Winston rereads the note even though he risks detection in doing so. He then throws the note down the memory hole.

Now Winston's biggest problem lies in arranging to meet the girl whose sincerity he does not doubt. After reviewing a number of options—all unworkable—Winston decides that the canteen at work is the best place to meet her again.

A week passes. Winston has no idea what has happened to the girl. The next day he sees her in the canteen and nearly succeeds in speaking to her, but he is invited to eat lunch at another table. He cannot safely refuse.

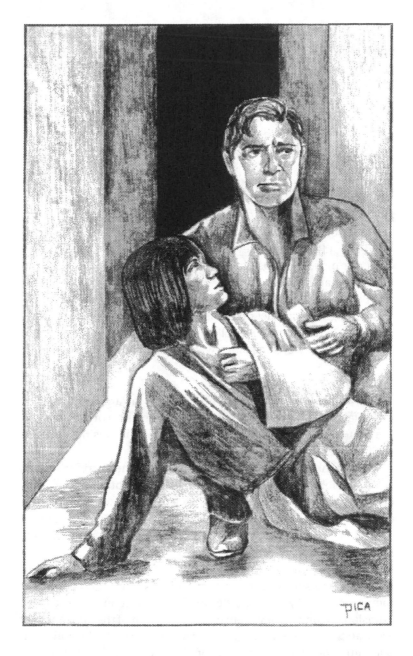

Finally, on the next day, they meet at work. Winston fears she has changed her mind, for things like this do not really happen. Despite the presence of numerous telescreens that might spot them, they plan to meet at 19 hours in Victory Square.

Winston is early for their appointment. Near the base of the monument to Big Brother stands the girl. They cannot approach one another until more people arrive.

Suddenly there is a huge shout and everyone rushes to the south side of the square to see a passing convoy of Eurasian prisoners. Winston and the girl position themselves in the middle of the crowd where they exchange a few brief words. The girl then gives Winston a series of directions to an outlying area where they will meet on Sunday.

To avoid detection they try to separate, but the curious crowd does not move. To those in Victory Square the foreigners are no more than animals on display.

Before the crowd gives way, the girl squeezes Winston's hand. Even though the contact only lasts ten seconds, Winston learns every detail of her hand. Ironically, Winston does not dare to look at the girl's eyes, for even a glance would mean certain punishment.

Analysis

Orwell continues to build the suspense toward the forbidden love affair. A week passes between the transmission of the note and the first meeting in Victory Square under the imposing statue of Big Brother.

Winston's reaction to the girl's distress in the corridor reveals his confusion over his basic humanity. "In front of him was an enemy who was trying to kill him; in front of him, also, was a human creature, in pain and perhaps with a broken bone." The reader should also recognize that when Winston receives the note, his reactions are of fear and mistrust.

Although Winston still retains a sense of the kinship within mankind, the same cannot be said for his comrades, the Party members. As they stand in Victory Square watching a convoy of Eurasian prisoners, they seem to have lost sight of the fact that they are watching fellow human beings suffering public humiliation. Such attitudes are reminiscent of Nazi Germany. Orwell writes,

"The prevailing emotion was of simple curiosity. Foreigners, whether from Eurasia or from Eastasia, were a kind of strange animal."

Winston's feelings and actions here serve to differentiate him from the rest of the society in which he lives, a society grown immune to suffering and hatred, where little regard for human dignity remains.

Study Questions

1. How much time has passed since Winston spotted the girl from the Fiction Department outside the junk shop?

2. What conflicting emotions does Winston feel before helping the girl?

3. Give the possible sources of the note.

4. Give the message on the note.

5. Tell why Winston no longer believes the girl is an enemy.

6. Where do Winston and the girl plan to meet?

7. Tell what Winston and the girl witness in the square.

8. When and where will the couple meet again?

9. What emotion prevails when Party members see foreigners?

10. What does the girl do right before she leaves?

Answers

1. Four days have passed.

2. Winston feels apprehensive but concerned for the girl's well-being.

3. The note could have come from either the Thought Police or from the underground, as well as just from the girl herself.

4. The message was, "I love you."

5. Winston saw how frightened the girl was as she handed him the note.

6. They plan to meet in Victory Square, near the monument.

7. They witness a convoy of Eurasian prisoners.

8.   They will meet Sunday in a field somewhere outside the city.

9.   Curiosity prevails when Party members see foreigners.

10. The girl reaches for Winston's hand and squeezes it.

Suggested Essay Topics

1.   From the beginning, the circumstances surrounding this love affair suggest its doom. Explain how Winston first learns of Julia's interest in him. Detail their difficulties in arranging a meeting. Why can they not meet in the open? Why had Winston initially distrusted Julia, and why do his feelings change?

2.   Discuss Winston's fearing Julia while at the same time wanting to help her because she is a human being.

Part II, Chapter 2

Summary

After traveling a considerable distance, Winston arrives at the predesignated meeting spot. Although there are no telescreens, he worries about concealed microphones and patrolling soldiers who might check his passport.

The girl arrives and leads Winston to a clearing on a grassy knoll surrounded by trees. Winston worries about rejection, but the girl is not put off by his age, physical appearance, or marital status. They embrace and kiss but Winston has no physical desire for her. He merely feels incredulous over the entire experience.

Winston finally learns her name: Julia. He confesses that he had hated the sight of her, thinking she was a member of the Thought Police. Telling the truth as a love offering seems a good prelude to the affair. Julia, in response, rips off the scarlet sash around her waist, the symbol of the Junior Anti-Sex League. She offers Winston a small piece of chocolate she obtained through the black market. The smell provokes Winston to a vague recollection, but he cannot remember exactly why the odor should be so disturbing.

Julia confesses that the reason she had selected Winston was that she is good at spotting people who do not belong. Instinctively, she knows Winston is against the Party.

Arms intertwined, the couple strolls to the edge of the field where they will leave one another. Winston recognizes the field from the one in his recurring dream, the Golden Country. Somewhere a thrush is singing beautifully. Winston admires its freedom and beauty.

Winston and Julia return to the clearing where they make love. It is almost the same as Winston's dream. Julia admits to other lovers; in fact, she is quite proud of her numerous liaisons. She makes no attempt to hide her animal instinct, the one act of rebellion that could ruin the Party.

Analysis

The near impossibility of the affair's being consummated is made clear in the opening passages describing the roundabout route to the forbidden meeting, the hidden microphones, and patrolling soldiers. We are reminded of the caption "Big Brother Is Watching You," for it certainly appears that this is true. In view of these extensive preparations, Winston's earlier actions of washing the ink stains from his hands do not seem out-of-the-ordinary.

Winston's reaction to the gift of black-market chocolate suggests a repressed memory, a device Orwell uses to develop character. "But there was still that memory moving round the edges of his consciousness, something strongly felt but not reducible to definite shape, like an object seen out of the corner of one's eye. He pushed it away from him, aware only that it was the memory of some action which he would have liked to undo but could not."

Another recurrent motif is the dream. The setting for the first sexual encounter with Julia mirrors the setting in Winston's dream of the Golden Country. The thrush's exuberant song represents freedom and spontaneity. Marvelling at its song, Winston watches with "vague reverence." As with the girl in the dream, Winston admires Julia's independence and spontaneity. Orwell says, "...when she flung them aside it was with that same magnificent gesture by which a whole civilization seemed to be annihilated." Similarly, before they make love, Julia flings aside the red sash around her waist, a symbol of chastity for the Junior Anti-Sex League.

Winston's reaction to the news of Julia's numerous lovers hardly shocks us in view of the Party's doctrine, already explained as: "Its real, undeclared purpose was to remove all pleasure from the sexual act. Not love so much as eroticism was the enemy, inside of marriage as well as outside it."

Julia reveals not only her independence but also her honesty as she admits to being absolutely corrupt. Initially, then, this affair begins for two different reasons. To Julia, the lovemaking is the culmination of their response to animal instincts. To Winston, however, their daring act becomes a political act of rebellion against the Party.

Study Questions

1. Tell why a person is no safer in the countryside than in London.

2. What does Winston confess?

3. What is Winston's immediate feeling as he holds Julia in his arms?

4. What is Winston's idea of a love offering?

5. What is the emblem of the Junior Anti-Sex League?

6. Where did Julia obtain the chocolate?

7. What has attracted Julia to Winston?

8. Why is Winston shocked at the coarseness of Julia's language?

9. What is Julia's feeling about her many other lovers?

10. What is the one act of rebellion that could ruin the Party?

Answers

1. A person's voice might be picked up by hidden microphone or his passport might be checked.

2. Winston confesses to his age, marital status, and his physical condition. He also admits that at first he thought she was a member of the Thought Police.

3. Winston's immediate feeling is incredulity.

4. Winston's idea of a love offering is to start off telling the truth.

5. The emblem is a scarlet sash worn about the waist.

6. Julia had obtained the chocolate from the black market.

7. Julia is attracted to Winston because she sensed something different about him, and that he was against the Party.

8. Winston is shocked because Party members do not use profanity.

9. Julia is proud of her many lovers.

10. The act of rebellion that could ruin the Party is acting on animal instincts.

Suggested Essay Topics

1. Orwell makes use of several symbols here, especially those occurring in Winston's dream of the Golden Country. List and explain the common elements in the dream and in Winston and Julia's first sexual encounter. Focus especially on the landscape, the girl's gesture, and the thrush as symbols.

2. Explain how the establishment of a relationship between Winston and Julia has many levels of meaning—personal, political, etc.

Part II, Chapter 3

Summary

During the next few weeks Julia and Winston make love only once, in a ruined church Julia knows. Since meeting is so dangerous, sometimes after arriving at a spot the most they can do is exchange glances. Time is a problem as well, since so many evenings are devoted to Party activities.

Winston learns more about Julia. She is 26 years old; she lives in a hostel with 30 other women, and she works on the novel-writing machines in the Fiction Department. By her own admission she is not intelligent. Although she enjoys the process of creating books, she has little regard for reading them.

Julia remembers nothing prior to the early sixties. She is well-regarded at work, having been selected to work in Pornosec, the subdivision of the Fiction Department which produces cheap pornography for the proles.

To Julia, life is simple. She believes in having a good time and finds it necessary to break Party rules in order to do so. She hates the Party because it has infringed on her personal freedoms, but she seems disinterested in Party doctrine or in an organized Revolution.

The couple realizes the impossibility of marriage because the Party would never sanction such a union. Besides, Winston is already married. He tells Julia the details of his marriage to Katharine and her outlook on their sexual relations.

Julia, however, already knows the details since she too had been schooled by these monthly sex talks, a standard for all girls over 16. Unlike Katharine, however, Julia has rejected the Party's teachings. Everything revolves around her own sexuality. She understands that the Party can make use of their sexual privation, as frustrations increase the zest for war and hero worship.

Winston agrees. The Party had used repressed sexual impulses to its advantage and the impulse towards parenthood for its own benefit. Children spy on their parents and turn them in to the Thought Police routinely. In this way everyone is watched night and day.

On one point Julia and Winston disagree. She does not accept as inevitable the fact that the individual is doomed. She believes in a secret world where one can express his or her individuality. Winston, however, prefers to consider themselves dead, for happiness only occurs in the distant future long after death.

Analysis

The character of Julia dominates this chapter. Although she claims not "to be clever," she reveals her cunning in a number of different ways. She is the one who plans the secret rendezvous sites and who immerses herself in Party activities so she will be least suspected of breaking the rules.

Julia is also independent. She hates the Party, which she describes with a number of profanities. Her independence does not stem from ideological differences with the Party; her aim in life is to have a good time, and the Party is preventing this.

Orwell explores the basic instinct of sexuality through Julia, for whom everything stems from that instinct. In this area she is far more intelligent than Winston. Unlike Winston, she realized the true meaning of the Party's puritanical stance on the issue of sexuality. It was not only that the sex instinct needed to be repressed if possible in order for the Party to maintain control; but, "What was more important was that sexual privation induced hysteria, which was desirable because it could be transformed into war fever and leader worship." Later, the behavior of Party members prior to Hate Week seems to support Julia's view. We should also remember that Orwell wrote this novel during wartime England, when patriotism definitely played a major part in British life.

Like the thrush that sang so beautifully in the meadow, Julia represents hope and spontaneity. Although logic tells her that she and Winston are doomed, she earnestly believes in the ability to live in a secret world where one can be free. As Julia says so directly, "All you needed was luck and cunning and boldness." Thus far, Julia has demonstrated that she possesses all three of these characteristics.

Study Questions

1. Tell why Winston does not need to know Julia's surname or address.

2. What does Julia mean by "talking in installments"?

3. How does Julia spend much of her free time?

4. What does Julia do at the Fiction Department?

5. What special job was Julia selected for at work?

6. What is Julia's only interest in Party doctrine?

7. Give Julia's opinion of revolt against the Party.

8. What is Julia's reaction when Winston tells her the details of his loveless marriage?

9. According to Julia, what does sexual privation produce?

10. What does Julia believe will help Winston and her to construct a secret world in which they can live?

Answers

1. Winston does not need this information because it is unlikely he and Julia could ever meet indoors or exchange letters through the mail.

2. Julia is referring to furtive conversations interrupted by the presence of telescreens or patrols.

3. Julia spends much of her free time in Party-related activities.

4. Julia services the electric motors of the novel-writing machines in the Fiction Department.

5. Julia had been selected to work in Pornosec.

6. Julia was only interested in Party doctrine when it directly affected her.

7. Julia thought a revolt would be stupid and doomed to failure.

8. Julia is not surprised at these details.

9. According to Julia, sexual privation produces a hysteria which could be channeled into war fever and hero worship.

10. Julia believes luck, cunning, and boldness can help her and Winston construct a secret world.

Suggested Essay Topics

1. Orwell has placed major emphasis on the character of Julia in this chapter. Evaluate her statement that she is "not clever." What evidence refutes this statement?

2. What does Julia's position on Party doctrine reveal? How does this position contrast with Winston's views?

Part II, Chapter 4

Summary

Winston rents the room above the junk shop. Mr. Charrington, who is obviously glad about the rent, seems unaffected by the fact that the room will be used for a secret affair.

Winston's paperweight sits on the table. He has brought some

Victory Coffee and saccharine. The clock on the mantelpiece reads 7:20, but it is really 19:20 in the outside world.

From the courtyard a solid-looking prole woman sings as she hangs the laundry on the clothesline. She is singing a melody created just weeks before by a versificator in the Music Department. To Winston, the melody, combined with the usual sounds of the neighborhood, seems delightful. Despite the noise, however, without a telescreen the room seems to echo.

Julia arrives with a number of items usually possessed by Inner Party members: sugar, bread, jam, milk, but most importantly, real coffee. Julia matter-of-factly announces that she has stolen these things from "those swine."

Julia surprises Winston by painting her face with makeup from a shop in the proletarian section. Even though she is not very skillful, Winston appreciates the difference in her appearance since Party women are not allowed to wear makeup. They undress and make love. Julia has never been in a double bed, an uncommon sight except in the homes of proles.

After a brief nap they awaken to prepare some coffee. Winston is due back at his apartment by 23:30. Suddenly Julia flings a shoe into the corner of the room where a rat is about to enter through a hole in the bottom of the wall. Julia seems unaffected by the rat's intrusion, but Winston clenches his eyes shut in terror.

Winston recalls another recurring nightmare. In this dream, he stands before a wall of darkness; behind the wall is something dreadful, but unknown. He does not confide in Julia but dismisses the incident with the words, "It's nothing, I don't like rats, that's all."

Julia fixes a snack and they prepare to leave. She picks up the paperweight and asks Winston what it is. Winston tells her that the coral is a piece of history that the Party has forgotten to alter.

Julia examines the picture on the wall. Winston identifies the building in it as a church, St. Clement's Dane. Wistfully, he again remembers the fragments of the nursery rhyme: "Oranges and lemons, say the bells of St. Clement's."

Surprisingly, Julia remembers the next two lines, which she had learned from her grandfather who had been vaporized when she was eight. The two speculate on the lemons and oranges, which have become an uncommon sight.

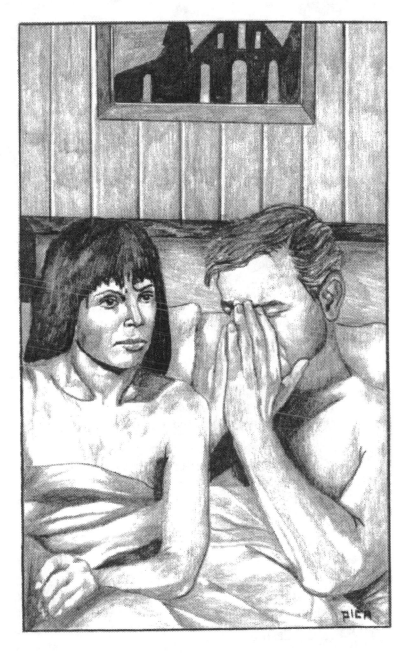

As the room darkens, Winston stares into the paperweight. To him, the surface of the glass becomes the arch of the sky, which encloses its own tiny world. The coral then becomes his and Julia's life together.

Analysis

In this chapter Winston and Julia attempt to construct a "secret world," and, at least for now, they appear to have succeeded. The clock set at 7:30, unlike those of the outside world, suggests a world and a time entirely their own. In the last month the room has become a refuge against the increased hatred in Oceania as its citizens prepare for Hate Week. Orwell suggests, however, that this happiness is short-lived when he says, "It was as though they were intentionally stepping nearer to their graves."

Orwell also employs foreshadowing when a rat invades the sanctuary. Julia, in her typical pragmatic fashion, throws a shoe at the vermin but Winston reacts differently:

> For several moments he had had the feeling of being back in a nightmare which had recurred from time to time throughout his life. It was always very much the same. He was standing in front of a wall of darkness, and on the other side of it there was something unendurable, something too dreadful to be faced.

Winston's paperweight takes on two additional meanings here. As Winston explains to Julia, the paperweight is a piece of the past the Party has forgotten to alter. On a symbolic level the artifact, with its solid core and domed sky, has come to represent safety and refuge, the dominant ideas of this chapter.

Study Questions

1. What does Winston's heart keep saying about the affair?
2. What does Winston see and hear under the window?
3. What is Winston thinking of as he awaits Julia?
4. What has Julia brought?

5. What does Winston see when he faces Julia?

6. Why does Julia throw a shoe into the corner?

7. What is Winston's reaction when Julia describes the rat?

8. What is Winston's opinion of the paperweight?

9. According to Winston, who might know the missing line to the nursery rhyme?

10. What has the paperweight come to symbolize for Winston?

Answers

1. Winston's heart tells him the affair is suicide.

2. Winston sees and hears a huge prole woman who is singing as she hangs the laundry to dry.

3. Winston has been thinking of the surety of the cellars of the Ministry of Love.

4. Julia has brought coffee, sugar, bread, jam, and milk.

5. Winston sees that Julia is wearing make-up.

6. Julia throws a shoe at an intrusive rat.

7. Winston feels as if he were back in a nightmare.

8. Winston believes that the paperweight is a piece of history the Party has been unable to alter.

9. Charrington may know the missing line.

10. To Winston, the paperweight has come to symbolize his shared life with Julia inside the room.

Suggested Essay Topics

1. The coral paperweight becomes a major symbol in this novel. When Julia asks about the paperweight, how does Winston explain its significance? What has the paperweight come to symbolize to Winston himself? Give evidence to support the fact that the room, like the paperweight, has become a sanctuary or refuge for Winston and Julia.

2. Discuss Winston's reaction to the peasant woman's song.
    What is ironic about its source? What additional qualities of
    the peasant woman does Winston admire?

Part II, Chapter 5

Summary

   Syme vanishes, almost as if he had never existed.

   Meanwhile, preparations for Hate Week continue. Julia's department is publishing a series of atrocity pamphlets. Winston
spends part of his work day altering sections of old news stories
that will be quoted in the latest speeches. The bombings of the city
grow more frequent.

   New posters that have no caption but show a large Eurasian
soldier holding a submachine gun appear all over; wherever one
goes the gun seems to follow. These posters seem to outnumber
even those of Big Brother. Accompanied by the incessant bombing of innocent children, these posters foster an air of patriotism
amidst the chaos of the city.

   In the room over Charrington's shop, Julia and Winston are in
paradise. Even the ever-present bugs do not bother them. They
meet several times during June.

   The changes in Winston are dramatic. He has stopped drinking gin; he has gained weight; and his varicose ulcer has healed.
He and Julia treasure this secret hiding place; just knowing it is
theirs is a constant source of happiness. Although they know the
affair is bound to end, as long as they have the room they feel no
harm will come.

   Sometimes they talk about rebellion against the Party, but
neither has any idea of how to put their plans into action. They are
not even sure that the Brotherhood exists, or how they could get
into it. Winston considers approaching O'Brien, with whom he
shares a strange affinity.

   Although Julia takes for granted that everyone hates the Party
and would break its rules willingly, she refuses to believe that a
widespread, organized opposition such as the Brotherhood exists.
In fact, she claims the tales of Goldstein have been concocted by

the Party for its own benefit. Too young to remember anything before the Revolution, she cannot conceive of such a thing as an independent political movement.

In Julia's opinion the war against Eurasia is not happening and the government of Oceania is bombing its own citizens to keep them frightened.

Winston tells her about the forgeries he creates at the Records Department, but she is unconcerned. He tries to tell her the story of Jones, Aaronson, and Rutherford, but she fails to understand his point. Winston continues; he is concerned that the past is being abolished with every record being falsified or destroyed, every book being rewritten. Winston worries that all that exists is a present time in which the Party is always right. The only evidence of the past is in his own mind. Julia counters that she is interested in neither the past nor the present—just in them.

Julia has the annoying habit of falling asleep when Winston tries to talk about Party doctrine, the principles of Ingsoc, doublethink, or the mutability of the past. Through her, Winston realizes how easy it is to present the outward appearance of the devoted Party member while having no inward idea of what the Party ideology conveys.

Analysis

Ironically, by being vaporized, Syme becomes an "unperson," stripped of his identity by a word of his own creation.

The contrast between the increased tensions prior to Hate Week and the peace and contentment in the room over Charrington's shop is quite apparent. We are reminded of Julia's earlier remarks on the effects of sexual privation as the frenzy over Hate Week accelerates. Parsons, with the odor of his sweat even more pronounced, seems absolutely tireless as he leads the Party preparations, thus reinforcing the idea that it is not difficult for the unintelligent to be leaders. The poster of the Eurasian soldier seems to mock Big Brother, and the deaths of innocent children heighten emotions.

In contrast, in the room over Charrington's shop all seems well as Winston and Julia dare to dream of escape even though freedom is unlikely. When we see the physical changes in Winston and his increased sense of well-being, we see the correlation between one's physical and emotional health that Julia has alluded to earlier.

Winston remains curious about the existence of an underground Brotherhood, but Julia voices an opinion that Winston has not quite dared to think. She believes Goldstein and the war are both creations of the Party, designed to further the cause of patriotism. In view of this, her admission to laughter during the Two Minutes Hate is thoroughly in line with her character.

The ability of the Party to manipulate seems to have credence here—Julia remembers nothing before the Revolution, and she does not realize that only four short years ago Oceania had been at war with Eastasia.

Orwell attacks the blindness of the masses in the chapter's final analogy: "By lack of understanding they remained sane. They simply swallowed everything, and what they swallowed did them no harm, because it left no residue behind, just as a grain of corn will pass undigested through the body of a bird."

Study Questions

1. Who vanishes?

2. How is Winston preparing for Hate Week at work?

3. Who organizes the squads of volunteers?

4. What is pictured on the new poster appearing all over London?

5. What causes the proles to feel increasingly patriotic?

6. How does Winston regard the room over Charrington's shop?

7. What does Julia take for granted?

8. What does Julia believe about the stories of Goldstein and the underground?

9. What is Julia's impulse during the Two Minutes Hate?

10. What is Julia's interest in the next generation?

Answers

1. Syme vanishes.
2. Winston is altering items from the back issues of the *Times*.
3. Tom Parsons organizes the volunteers.
4. The new poster pictures an Eurasian soldier pointing a submachine gun.
5. The proles feel more patriotic because there are more bombings than usual.
6. The room is a sanctuary where he and Julia are safe.
7. Julia takes for granted her belief that everyone hates the Party.
8. Julia believes these stories have been invented by the Party.
9. Her impulse is to laugh.
10. Julia is only interested in the present; the future, and the next generation, does not concern her.

Suggested Essay Topics

1. As the novel progresses, we see several physical changes in Winston. Describe these changes, and explain why Orwell believes they are happening. Contrast these changes and Winston's overall delight in the affair with the increasing mood of hatred as the preparations for Hate Week continue.
2. Contrast Winston's and Julia's attitudes toward Party doctrine, rebellion, and Big Brother. Tell why it is unlikely that Winston and Julia will ever successfully rebel.

Part II, Chapter 6

Summary

O'Brien approaches Winston at work to talk to him about one of his recent articles on Newspeak. O'Brien refers to a friend whose name happens to have slipped his mind who has a high opinion of Winston's work.

Winston thinks briefly of Syme, but Syme has been abolished, has become an "unperson." Still, Winston believes this remark was intended as a sort of signal. In sharing this small act of thoughtcrime, Winston and O'Brien become accomplices.

As they continue down the hall, O'Brien remarks that Winston has used two words that are now obsolete in Newspeak. He offers Winston a new tenth edition of the Newspeak dictionary—not yet readily available—suggesting that Winston might pick it up at his apartment.

In full view of the telescreen, O'Brien scribbles his address on paper and hands it to Winston. After memorizing the address, Winston throws the paper down the memory hole. Winston believes that O'Brien has contrived the meeting to let him know his address, since there are no directories of any sort.

Winston knows it is only a matter of time before he visits O'Brien. Frightened, he feels a chilling sensation passing through his body as he has the sensation of stepping into a grave.

Analysis

This chapter is a turning point in the novel. An anxious Winston is approached by O'Brien, who dupes him into committing "thoughtcrime" through veiled references to Syme. There is no substantial evidence, however, that O'Brien is an ally. Given the oppressiveness of Winston's work environment, though, we understand why Winston so eagerly accepts O'Brien as a potential accomplice.

The novel's underlying pessimism becomes more apparent. Despite his happiness at connecting with a purported member of the Brotherhood, Winston knows the consequences of these actions will come later in the Ministry of Love. Orwell foreshadows the conclusion when he says: "He had the sensation of stepping into the dampness of a grave, and it was not much better because he had always known that the grave was there and waiting for him." Once again, the futility of Winston's struggle against Big Brother is underscored.

Study Questions

1. Where is Winston when O'Brien approaches him?
2. How does O'Brien compliment Winston?

3. Why does O'Brien refer to Syme only indirectly?

4. How does O'Brien turn Winston into his accomplice?

5. What does O'Brien think is an ingenious development in the tenth edition of the Newspeak dictionary?

6. What is O'Brien willing to lend Winston?

7. What happens to the paper with the address?

8. What prevents Winston from finding out O'Brien's address on his own?

9. What is the one thing of which Winston is now certain?

10. What feeling does Winston experience as he talks with O'Brien?

Answers

1. Winston is in the corridor at the Ministry of Truth.

2. O'Brien compliments Winston on his knowledge of Newspeak.

3. A direct reference to Syme would have been dangerous, because Syme is now an "unperson."

4. They become accomplices through veiled references to Syme.

5. O'Brien thinks the reduction in the number of verbs is an ingenious development.

6. O'Brien is willing to lend Winston the dictionary.

7. Winston throws the paper down the memory hole.

8. Winston is prevented from finding the address because there are no directories in Oceania.

9. Winston is certain that a conspiracy against the Brotherhood does exist.

10. Winston experiences a chilling, shuddering feeling.

Suggested Essay Topics

1. In many respects, O'Brien is the most important character in the novel, although at this point Orwell has not characterized him with the same depth as either Winston or Julia.

On what pretense does O'Brien approach Winston? What inferences suggest that O'Brien might be less than honest? What concrete evidence does Winston have that a Brotherhood does exist?

2. What is foreshadowed by the chilling sensation Winston feels as he talks with O'Brien? Besides fear, what other emotions might have provoked these sensations?

Part II, Chapter 7

Summary

Awakening from yet another dream, Winston remembers his last glimpse of his mother and the circumstances of her disappearance. For the first time he clearly remembers these events, which had been deliberately suppressed for years.

Winston remembers childhood afternoons spent scavenging the garbage bins for scraps. Even his father had been unable to fulfill his role as provider; Winston's most vivid memory of him is of his thin-soled shoes. After his father's disappearance, Winston's mother had merely gone through the motions of housekeeping and child care (a woman's role at that time); she seemed to be waiting for something to happen.

After a lapse of some weeks, a chocolate ration had been issued. The meager two ounces was meant to be divided into three equal parts, but young Winston had put up quite a fight for more than his share despite his mother's repeated requests that he consider his younger sister. Finally, she gave most of the chocolate to Winston, who also snatched his sister's portion before running from the apartment. As he reached out for the candy, Winston's mother instinctively had put her arm around his sister in a protective gesture.

Later, when he was again hungry, Winston had returned to the apartment, but his mother and ailing sister were gone. Even today, he does not really know what happened to them.

With this dream so vivid, especially the picture of the protective gesture of his mother's arm, Winston is reminded of a prior dream in which his mother and sister are on a sinking ship. His mother had had the same protective gesture then.

Winston confides in Julia, but she is not much interested except to observe that Winston, like all other children, must have been a swine.

Winston continues to think lovingly of his mother and the gesture. Even though it had not changed a thing, the natural impulsive gesture had meant something. Winston then thinks about the Party, which has done so much to persuade people that impulses and feelings are not important. In the Party's grip, feelings make no difference, and regardless of what had happened, a person vanished, never to be heard from again.

Winston thinks of how things have changed. People like his mother had been guided by private loyalties, not loyalties to the whole. These musings lead Winston to think enviously of the proles who, in his opinion, had stayed human, holding onto primitive emotions that Winston is only now relearning through his affair with Julia. His mind wanders to the human hand that only weeks ago he had kicked so mindlessly into the gutter.

Winston senses that their luck is about to run out and when it does, regardless of any confession, they will be shot. Winston hopes they will not betray one another.

Julia accepts the fact that they will both confess, but the real betrayal, they both agree, would come only if the Party could make them stop loving one another. Julia and Winston agree on one more point: the Party cannot get inside them.

Analysis

Orwell returns to the function of dreams in this chapter as, for the first time, Winston fully understands the circumstances surrounding his mother's disappearance and the intense feelings she had had for both of her children. These memories, repressed for years, allow Winston to confront his past.

As Winston awakens, he imagines the dream to have taken place under the dome of the sky, like the dome of the paperweight, its events bathed in a soft light, symbolically the light of understanding. The protective gesture his mother made while Winston stole his sister's chocolate ration echoes the one she made in the dream of the sinking ship. Winston realizes this is the same gesture a Jewish woman had made on film immediately before she and a young boy were blown up. Even though the Jewish woman and Winston's mother are separated by time and place (Hitler's Germany and Stalin's Russia), they share a common emotion: love and the desire to protect loved ones.

Winston believes that only the proles have retained the basic emotions that make them human; unlike Party members, who are, in a sense, already dead. As he discusses the implications of these views with Julia, she offers the hope that the Party cannot divest a person of his or her thoughts. Julia believes that although the love affair will end and they will both confess, they will not have betrayed one another, for real betrayal can come only when they have stopped loving one another.

Julia's opinion, contrasted against a background of despair, reflects her belief in the dignity and goodness of the human spirit, for she truly believes that their object is to stay human, not necessarily to stay alive.

Study Questions

1. What do the arm gestures made by Winston's mother in the dreams have in common with one another?

2. What does Winston remember in his dream?

3. What does Winston believe the proles have retained, but Party members have lost?

4. How did Winston spend many of his childhood afternoons?

5. How did Winston's mother react to her husband's disappearance?

6. What did Winston do with his sister's portion of the chocolate ration?

7. What did Winston find when he returned home?

8. What is a Reclamation Center?

9. In Winston's mind, what would prove he had betrayed Julia?

10. According to Julia, what is the one thing the Party cannot do?

Answers

1. They were gestures of protection.

2. Winston had remembered his last glimpse of his mother.

3. Winston believes the proles have retained ordinary human emotions, yet Party members have not.

4. Winston spent many afternoons looking through garbage bins for food.

5. Winston's mother only went through the motions of house-keeping and childrearing.

6. Winston stole his sister's portion of the chocolate ration.

7. When he returned home, Winston discovered that his mother and sister were gone.

8. A Reclamation Center is a colony for homeless children.

9. Winston's betrayal of Julia will occur when he stops loving her.

10. Julia believes the Party cannot get inside a person.

Suggested Essay Topics

1. Orwell interweaves the themes of betrayal and hope in this critical chapter. Discuss how Winston has arrived at his conclusion that the hope for the future lies in the proles. What has Winston learned about universal human emotions from his dreams? What belief dominates Winston and Julia's belief that they will not betray one another?

2. Discuss the additional insights into his mother's feelings for her family that Winston gains from his latest dreams of her disappearance.

Part II, Chapter 8

New Character:

Martin: *O'Brien's servant*

Summary

After taking separate routes to avoid detection, Winston and Julia arrive at O'Brien's apartment, where they are admitted by the servant, Martin.

For a moment, Winston feels embarrassed and somewhat stupid for believing O'Brien to be a political ally without any substantial proof.

O'Brien turns off the telescreen, a privilege granted only to Inner Party members. Confessing that he believes O'Brien is involved in the underground, Winston expresses a wish to join. He admits that he and Julia are thoughtcriminals and adulterers. He tells O'Brien they want to put themselves at his mercy.

After Martin serves wine, they all drink a toast to Emmanuel Goldstein, leader of the Brotherhood. O'Brien asks a litany of questions to determine Winston's commitment to revolt. Winston says he is prepared to murder, kill the innocent, lose his identity, even to commit suicide. But when asked whether they are prepared to separate and never see one another again, it is Julia who answers first, "No."

O'Brien seems pleased with their honesty. He warns them that they will always be in the dark about their orders, which will come directly from him. He promises to send them a book with strategies to destroy the Party. Then they will become official members of the Brotherhood.

Although O'Brien recognizes that Winston and Julia will most likely be caught by the Party, he also says the Brotherhood is based on ideas, and ideas are indestructible.

Before Julia leaves, they drink a second toast, this time, to the past. Later, O'Brien makes arrangements to send Goldstein's book to Winston. O'Brien reassures Winston that they will meet again. Winston finishes with the phrase from the dream: "In the place where there is no darkness," and O'Brien seems to agree.

Analysis

The reader should wonder why a person of Winston's perception and intuition so easily accepts O'Brien as a member of the Brotherhood. Winston's eagerness here underscores his despera-

tion. Although the litany of crimes that Winston is all-too-willing to commit reinforces the hopelessness of his existence, O'Brien's method of interrogation is hypnotic. Note that it is Julia who interjects that she is not willing to accept a permanent separation from Winston, raising the question of what Winston's response would have been.

O'Brien's explanation of the Brotherhood is equally mysterious, for he tells Winston he will "always be in the dark." The circumstances of Winston's life seem bleak indeed, as O'Brien points out that change will not occur during his lifetime, and Winston's actions are certain to end in arrest, torture, and death. The statement "We are the dead" is both cryptic and prophetic.

Two factors especially lend a surrealistic quality to the meeting. O'Brien assures Winston that they will definitely meet, "In the place where there is no darkness," echoing the suggestion introduced earlier. In addition, Winston finally learns the last line of the nursery rhyme, "Oranges and lemons, say the bells of St. Clement's," which has so haunted him. He willingly accepts this remnant of an innocent past from O'Brien.

Study Questions

1. What does Winston fear as he travels to O'Brien's apartment?

2. What is the only evidence that suggests O'Brien is a political conspirator?

3. Why can Winston not use the excuse that he had come for the dictionary?

4. What privilege is reserved for Party members?

5. To whom does the group drink a toast?

6. According to O'Brien, what is the most Winston will ever know about the Brotherhood?

7. What is Winston prepared to do for the Brotherhood?

8. Why will the Brotherhood never be destroyed?

9. What is in the book that O'Brien plans to send to Winston?

10. Where will O'Brien and Winston meet again?

Answers

1. Winston fears that guards will check his papers and send him home.

2. The sole pieces of evidence are an expression in O'Brien's eyes and a single remark.

3. Winston cannot explain Julia's presence.

4. Inner Party members are allowed to turn off their telescreens.

5. They drink a toast to their leader, Emmanuel Goldstein.

6. Winston will only know that the Brotherhood exists.

7. Winston says he is willing to do anything for the Brotherhood.

8. The Brotherhood is held together by an idea that is indestructible.

9. The book contains Goldstein's message.

10. They will meet "in the place where there is no darkness."

Suggested Essay Topics

1. How Winston so easily accepts O'Brien as a political conspirator is a problem for readers who accept his intelligence and intuitiveness. Analyze the reasons for Winston's willingness to believe in O'Brien. What details imply that O'Brien is not what he seems?

2. Discuss the implications of the recurring phrase "...place where there is no darkness," versus O'Brien's statement that Winston will "always be in the dark."

Part II, Chapter 9

Summary

Having worked over 90 hours in the past few days, a fatigued Winston makes his way to the hideout at Charrington's shop with Goldstein's book. Winston is thinking about the sixth day of Hate Week when, after numerous activities designed to increase hatred of Eurasia, the Party has announced that Oceania is at war with Eastasia and that Eurasia is an ally. After the announcement Winston spent much of the next week rectifying the political literature of the last five years. By the end of the sixth day, no documentary evidence of the war with Eurasia remains.

Upon arriving at Charrington's shop, Winston begins the book *The Theory and Practice of Oligarchical Collectivism*. Chapter One, "Ignorance Is Strength," asserts that the goals of the three classes— High, Middle, and Low—contradict one another.

Winston, who is delighted with the freedom to read, now skips to Chapter Three, "War Is Peace." This chapter details the locations of the three superpowers who have been permanently at war for the last 25 years. The book characterizes war as occurring without motive since, with the advent of self-contained economies, there is no reason to fight. The main purpose of war is to use the surplus of consumer products without raising the standard of living for everyone. When all are satisfied, wealth as a symbol of distinction means nothing. Moreover, once poverty has become nonexistent, people learn to think for themselves and realize there is no need for a privileged minority. Thus, in order to maintain a hierarchical society, poverty and ignorance must exist.

War, which accomplishes destruction in a psychologically acceptable way, provides a basis for fear and hatred. All members of the Inner Party believe that war terminates in conquest, perhaps resulting from the discovery of a new weapon. All three powers, for example, possess the atomic bomb which is the most powerful weapon. After the first atomic bombs were exploded, the superpowers became frightened, produced no more, and stored the remainder for the day when the inevitable would occur.

Usually, large-scale campaigns involve surprise attacks on an ally. Once an area is surrounded with a ring of bases, the powers sign a friendship pact to remain allies, but, in the meantime, a strategic missile build-up is ongoing.

No fighting ever occurs except in some disputed areas; there is never an invasion of enemy territory lest the soldiers discover that the conquered foreigners are fellow human beings.

Philosophies—in all three states are almost the same—Ingsoc (Oceania); Neo-Bolshevism (Eurasia): and Obliteration of the Self

(Eastasia). Key concepts to all philosophies are:

1. pyramidical structures
2. worship of a semi-divine leader
3. economy geared toward war

With each of the three states becoming unconquerable, any ideological perversion can be made absolute.

Therefore, the previously held concept of war occurring because of some provocation no longer exists. In fact, permanent peace would be the same as permanent war; it has the same effects. This concept is the real meaning of the tenet "War Is Peace."

Winston is not surprised by what he reads. After Julia arrives and they make love, he begins to read aloud Chapter One, "Ignorance Is Strength," which begins with an overview of the class system with one underlying constant; history shows a recurring series of clashes for power with the low class remaining low.

By the late nineteenth century, the book claims, these patterns had become apparent but were of no real concern since historians had declared them as cyclical. Even variants of Socialism after 1900 aimed less and less for liberty and equality, but, instead, aimed for *un*freedom and *in*equality.

By the beginning of the twentieth century, there was no longer any reason for social or economic class distinction because machines had made a life of productivity and leisure possible for everyone. Although the descendants affected by the French, English, and American revolutions may have believed in equality, by the 1930s political thought had changed and a hierarchy had become desirable. This thinking explains how long-abandoned practices such as trial, torture, and public executions became more widespread.

The new totalitarianism had leaders whose origins were in the salaried and upper middle class; therefore, wealth meant little to them, but power meant everything. Perhaps this interest in power stemmed from the fact that it became easier to control opinion via print and television.

In this setting the high class knew how to maintain its power, for it relied on the principle that oligarchy is collectivism, that wealth and privilege can be defended when they are possessed jointly.

The real effect, though, is that when the principle of private property is abolished, the real control is in the hands of a few. Collectively the Party owns everything in Oceania, but the decisions are made by a few. Ingsoc, based on this Socialist idea, resulted in a permanent economic inequality.

The book outlines the ways to perpetuate the hierarchical society whose ruling group can only fall from power under the following circumstances:

1. defeat from the outside

2. inefficiency causing the masses to revolt

3. allowing the discontented Middle to gain strength

4. losing its desire to rule

Most importantly, the mental attitude of the ruling group is crucial to its success.

In Oceania the perpetuation of the hierarchy is due to the persistence of the belief through children. One becomes an Inner or Outer Party member at age 16 after taking an exam. The proles really are no threat since their world has been shaped by the Party. They need no education, since military and commercial rivalries no longer exist and they have no intellect.

Commitment to the Party, combined with hatred of the enemy, shapes the life of every Party member, who has been taught from the earliest ages the skill of "crimestop," the faculty of stopping any dangerous thought. The need for flexibility in dealing with facts demands their continuous alteration made possible by "doublethink."

Since mutability of the past is the central tenet of Ingsoc, "doublethink" becomes critical because the Party seems to have a firmness of purpose associated with honesty. Under the guise of straightforwardness, the Party has deviously altered events in accordance with its philosophy. Thus, the Party has been able to stop history.

The linking together of opposites is the distinguishing feature of Oceania's society. Therefore, in the name of Socialism, the Party rejects its underlying principles. Even the major institutions are examples of "doublethink":

1. The society undermines family but preaches family loyalty to Big Brother.

2. Ministry of Peace concerns itself with war.

3. Ministry of Truth disseminates lies.

4. Ministry of Love is in charge of torture.

5. Ministry of Plenty oversees starvation.

As he concludes Chapter One, Goldstein asks the same question that has continued to bother Winston throughout the reading: Why should history be stopped at this particular time to avert human equality? Goldstein seems as perplexed as Winston.

At this point Winston realizes that he has not really learned anything new from either chapter. He understands "how"; he does not understand "why." At least, though, Winston feels somewhat comforted for he knows he is neither insane nor alone.

Analysis

Set against a background of oppression, Winston's joy at the freedom to read arouses the reader's curiosity as well. The first chapter of *The Theory and Practice of Oligarchical Collectivism* parodies Marx and Engels's *Communist Manifesto* (1848), which explains a recurrent pattern of a class struggle between the proletarians and bourgeois, the concept of economic determinism, and the inevitability of communism. That these ideas foreshadowed Stalin's totalitarianism is widely acknowledged.

The definition of Stalin's totalitarianism is caricatured as well; specifically, the belief in a hierarchical system with a semi-divine leader, Big Brother, who represents Joseph Stalin.

Orwell uses the vehicle of Goldstein's book to satirize several related concepts:

1. Indoctrination of youth by Hitler's Youth Groups and Soviet Young Pioneers—illustrated by Goldstein's explanation of admission to the Party at the age of 16 through exam

2. The accepted concept of rewriting history common to Stalin's Russia and other societies as well—illustrated in the discussion of the desirability of mutability of the past

3. Disillusionment with socialism—illustrated by Goldstein's statement that the Party strives for *un*equality

Goldstein's book also details the arms race, and although Orwell lived before the development of thermonuclear weapons, his vision is frightening and prophetic. He describes a typical campaign:

> During this time rockets loaded with atomic bombs can be assembled at all strategic spots; finally they will all be fired simultaneously, with effects so devastating as to make retaliation impossible. It will then be time to sign a pact of friendship with the remaining world power, in preparation for another attack. This scheme, it is hardly necessary to say, is a mere daydream.

Symbolically, Winston falls asleep before Goldstein is about to answer the central question: "I understand HOW: I do not understand WHY," which will be addressed later in the novel. Although Winston does not get the answer to his most troubling dilemma, the reading at least proves to him that he is not insane, nor is he alone.

Study Questions

1. With what power is Oceania now at war?
2. What has Winston been doing for the past six days at the Ministry of Truth?
3. What is the title of Goldstein's book?
4. What are Goldstein's three classes?
5. What does Goldstein's book claim is the primary aim of modern warfare?
6. What is the only possible basis of a hierarchical society?
7. What are the two aims of the Party?
8. What happens to the most gifted proles?
9. Why must the past be altered?
10. Define doublethink.

Answers

1. Oceania is now at war with Eastasia.

2. Winston has been rectifying the political literature of the past.

3. The book is called *The Theory and Practice of Oligarchical Collectivism.*

4. The three classes are High, Middle, and Low.

5. The aim of war is to use up products without raising the standard of living.

6. A hierarchical society exists based on poverty and ignorance.

7. The Party aims to conquer the earth and to destroy the possibility of complete thought.

8. The most gifted proles are eliminated.

9. The past must be altered to safeguard the Party's infallibility.

10. Doublethink refers to the power of believing and accepting two contradictory ideas.

Suggested Essay Topics

1. What effect does the book have on Winston? What does he learn from reading it? What is the unanswered question? What does he learn about himself?

2. What is Julia's interest in the book? In view of the way Orwell has developed her character, are you surprised by her reaction? Why or why not?

Part II, Chapter 10

Summary

When Julia and Winston awaken to a cold room, it is 20:30. Winston looks from the window at the ever-present singing prole hanging the laundry below. Winston admires the sturdy peasant; in fact, to him she is beautiful. He thinks of all the people held apart by lies and hatred, yet possessing the same hopes and potential to overturn the world.

Winston suddenly feels convinced that he knows what Goldstein had written as his final message, that hope lies with the proles. Equality translates into sanity.

Winston reminds Julia of the thrush that sang so beautifully that first day they had met in the woods. Winston sees that everyone sings except the Party members. As a member of the Party, he feels dead, but Julia mocks him. From behind the picture comes another mocking voice. The painting crashes to the ground as a telescreen is revealed.

Soldiers intrude and one smashes the paperweight. Someone kicks Winston as he sees Julia double over in pain when she is punched. Flinging her over his shoulder, a soldier takes her from the room.

Winston remains alone with the soldiers. A younger, more authoritative Mr. Charrington steps into the room, and Winston realizes that for the first time he is staring directly at a member of the Thought Police.

Analysis

As Winston continues to mull over the unanswered question, he determines that the future must lie with the proles. He envies the proles' vitality, having likened Julia and himself to the dead. Here, at least, was hope, for Winston realizes that even though people may be separated by boundaries, wars, class distinctions or ideologies, they are basically the same.

This hope is short-lived as Julia and Winston are about to be betrayed. Their world literally crashes down on them. Completely unaware that Big Brother was watching them, they have commented on the beauty of the picture of St. Clement's Lane, which ironically masks a telescreen. The smashing of Winston's paperweight is symbolic as the affair abruptly ends. Although this event has always been anticipated, Winston is shocked at betrayal by Charrington, who is a member of the Thought Police.

Study Questions

1. What is the only way that the secret of the love affair would be passed on?

2. What occurs to Winston as he thinks of all people?

3. What does Winston conclude is Goldstein's final message?

4. According to Winston, what kind of world would the proles create?

5. What makes Winston believe that proles are immortal?

6. How does Winston think he and Julia can share in the future?

7. What is behind the picture on the wall?

8. What follows the voice?

9. What happens to Winston's paperweight?

10. What occurs to Winston as he looks at Charrington?

Answers

1. The secret is to be passed by word of mouth.

2. Winston realizes that all people are the same.

3. Winston thinks the message is that the future belongs to the proles.

4. The proles would create a world where equality would exist.

5. Winston thinks that the vitality of the proles would be passed from generation to generation.

6. Winston thinks they should keep their minds alive to pass on the news that two plus two make four.

7. Behind the picture is a telescreen.

8. The intrusion of soldiers follows the voice.

9. A soldier smashes the paperweight.

10. Winston realizes that he is looking directly at a member of the Thought Police.

Suggested Essay Topics

1. Many of the developments in this chapter revolve around Winston's newly-formed acceptance of the universality of all people. Explain how Winston comes to that realization.

How does the sight and sound of the prole woman affect Winston? Why does Winston believe that the future lies with the proles?

2. Tell how the events in this chapter are an extension of the "Big Brother Is Watching You" motif.

Part III

Part III, Chapter 1

New Character:

Ampleforth: *a poet*

Summary

Winston finds himself in a cold, barren cell, presumably in the Ministry of Love, with telescreens monitoring his every move. This is his second cell. He had shared the first one with several other prisoners, including Party prisoners and common criminals. The Party prisoners were obviously easily intimidated and controlled by the guards, who gave them all the dirty jobs. They never spoke to anyone, including one another, except for a reference to "room one-oh-one."

As Winston sits alone in his cell thinking of what lies in store, he thinks of O'Brien with hope, for perhaps the Brotherhood will send the razor blade before his next beating. Now Winston understands the meaning of the phrase "the place where there is no darkness." There are no windows so he cannot tell whether it is day or night; no clocks so he does not know what time it is—only rows and rows of porcelain bricks.

Winston's reverie is interrupted by the arrival of a prisoner, Ampleforth, who, Winston believes, might bear the razor blade— but this is not so. Ampleforth reveals his "crime": the inability to remove the word "God" from a line of poetry. The two men cease talking when Ampleforth is taken to Room 101.

To his surprise, Winston is joined by Parsons, who has been arrested for thoughtcrime, which Parsons believes had gotten hold of him without his realizing it. Before being taken away, Parsons claims to be proud of the daughter who denounced him.

A chinless man who reminds Winston of a rodent sits down. Next enters a tall, thin, mean-looking man; shocked, Winston realizes that the man is slowly starving to death. The chinless man realizes this as well and offers him a piece of bread. Suddenly a voice from the telescreen screams an order to drop the bread. Guards enter, beat the chinless man, and throw him across the room, as blood oozes everywhere. Humiliated, he takes his seat on the bench.

Next the guard turns to the skull-faced man. "Room 101," he orders. The skull-faced man, terrified, falls on his knees and begs for mercy—even agreeing to sign a confession to anything. Desperate, he tries to convince the soldiers to take the chinless man. After a struggle during which the man's fingers are broken, the guards drag him away.

Winston continues hoping for the arrival of the razor blade. In spite of his desire not to betray Julia, intellectually he knows that faced with beatings and torture, he probably will talk.

When the door opens, in walks O'Brien. For a moment, Winston hopes O'Brien is a fellow prisoner, but innately he realizes that this cannot be true. During the following beating, Winston's arm is disabled.

Analysis

As this section begins, Winston travels inside the Ministry of Love, which he had observed fearfully from his apartment at Victory Gardens in the opening chapter. The stark atmosphere, amplified by the "cold lights," echoes the coldness of the April wind earlier. Orwell now reveals the true meaning of the "place where there is no darkness," with a brightly lit, antiseptic looking room.

There is a reunion of sorts when Winston meets his comrade, Ampleforth. In a world of distortion it seems fitting that the poet should be imprisoned because he kept the word "God" in a line of Kipling's poetry to better suit its rhyme scheme. It is hardly surprising to next see the naive, but effusive, Parsons, whose denouncement has been foreshadowed through the savageness of his children. Orwell here attacks the indiscriminate arrest, torture, and execution of the oppressed, a common practice in pre-Revolutionary France and Spain.

Fear dominates as Winston witnesses the "chinless man" begging for mercy right before he is taken to the mysterious Room 101. Winston's fellow prisoners remain nameless to suggest their representative qualities. The "skull-faced" man becomes a coward pleading for his life, which is destined to end in the same way as those of his fellow prisoners. Orwell describes the scene: "The man looked frantically round at the other prisoners, as though with some idea that he could put another victim in his place." These words foreshadow Winston's ultimate act of betrayal when he too journeys to Room 101.

We see another form of betrayal in the character of O'Brien who, until this point, has symbolized Winston's hope that the Party can be undone. Like Charrington, however, he is not what he appears to be. Learning that O'Brien is a loyal member of the Inner Party only reinforces the overall hopelessness of Winston's struggle.

Study Questions

1. Where does Winston presume he is when he awakens?
2. What difference does Winston observe between Party prisoners and ordinary criminals?
3. Who does all the dirty jobs in the prisons?
4. Why does Winston think of O'Brien with hope?
5. What is the "place with no darkness"?
6. Why has Ampleforth been arrested?
7. Who has denounced Parsons?
8. What crime has Parsons committed?
9. What does the chinless man offer the skull-faced man?
10. Who is Winston's surprise visitor?

Answers

1. Winston presumes he is in the Ministry of Love.
2. Party prisoners are quiet and terrified, but the ordinary criminals do not care.
3. The dirty work is done by political prisoners.
4. Winston hopes O'Brien will send the razor blade.
5. The "place with no darkness" is the Ministry of Love.
6. Ampleforth has been unable to take the word "God" out of a line of poetry.
7. Parsons has been denounced by his daughter.
8. Parsons has committed thoughtcrime.
9. The chinless man offers a scrap of bread.
10. O'Brien is the surprise visitor.

Suggested Essay Topics

1. In this chapter we finally learn the full meaning of the recurrent phrase, "We shall meet in the place where there is no darkness." Explain the literal interpretation of this phrase. How might the phrase be interpreted symbolically? Under what circumstances was the phrase introduced early in the novel?

2. What is ironic about the function of the Ministry of Love?

Part III, Chapter 2

Summary

Winston, who continues to be regularly beaten, realizes that these beatings are only the beginning, a matter-of-course. The torture continues by Party members whose aim is to humiliate and belittle him through the use of constant traps and contradictions. This torture is supposed to destroy his power of reasoning.

Even the suggestion of a beating brings Winston to tears, and his only purpose in life now is to avoid a beating by confessing to whatever the Party seems to want—including crimes he could not have possibly committed.

Overhead, a light glares as Winston is strapped into a chair with several surrounding dials. Although he fades in and out of consciousness, he seems to think that O'Brien is in charge of the operation. The voice that whispers that it will save Winston is the same as the one that had whispered, "We shall meet in the place where there is no darkness."

As O'Brien stands over Winston, hand on a lever of a dial, he reminds Winston of his power as he delivers a jolt of electricity. The torturer suggests that Winston suffers from a defective memory. He points to the photo of Jones, Aaronson, and Rutherford that Winston has always believed validates their innocence. As O'Brien throws Winston's "hallucination" down the memory hole, he proclaims that it had never existed. Winston suspects that O'Brien has really forgotten the existence of the photo.

O'Brien reminds Winston once again of the Party slogan: "Who controls the past controls the future: who controls the present controls the past." Winston protests that even the Party cannot stop people from remembering things, but O'Brien disagrees, saying reality can only be looked at through the eyes of the Party. Winston, however, needs to humble himself before he can reach this point, which to the Party is sanity.

Holding his left hand with four fingers extended, O'Brien asks Winston to tell him the number of fingers he has raised. Winston answers, "Four," but O'Brien disagrees. Winston adheres to his belief, but every time he answers this question with "four" he is subjected to an electric shock. The jolts become progressively stronger until Winston finally capitulates with the answer, "Five."

An injection eases Winston's pain, but the games continue with O'Brien's telling Winston that he has been brought to this place to make him sane. The Party is not interested in the so-called crimes he has committed but in the thought process behind them. O'Brien tells Winston that when he gives in of his own free will, and undoubtedly he will, then he will be converted.

While speaking, he places a machine on Winston's head. "Three thousand," he hears right before a jolt passes through him. As a result, Winston now sees that Oceania has always been at war with

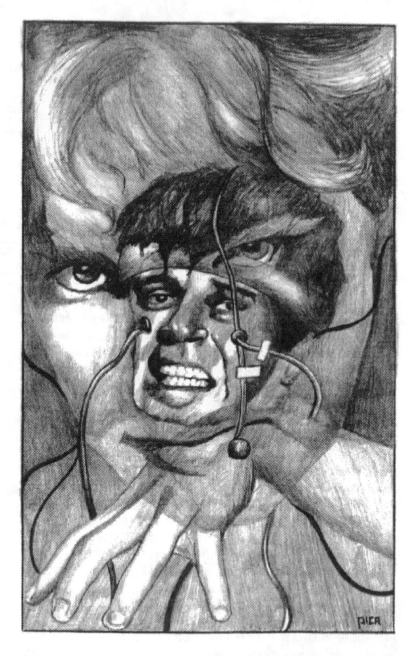

Eastasia, that he had invented the photo of Jones, Aaronson and Rutherford, and that O'Brien holds five fingers in the air.

Before the session ends, O'Brien allows Winston to ask a few questions. First, he asks about Julia, who supposedly has betrayed him. He then asks about the real existence of Big Brother, and O'Brien replies that their leader is an embodiment of Party principles. Winston asks about the Brotherhood, but O'Brien says he will never know more about it. Lastly, Winston asks about the contents of Room 101—but O'Brien counters that Winston already knows the answer.

The session over, Winston falls into a drug-induced sleep.

Analysis

Winston's physical torture is intense, but in many respects the mental degradation is worse. Some critics have likened O'Brien to Dostoyevski's Grand Inquisitor because of his desire for control and power with his willingness to inflict physical pain in the process. Orwell describes the joy he takes in Winston's interrogation as "a sort of exaltation, a lunatic intensity." As he plays a cat-and-mouse game with Winston's interrogation, O'Brien reveals both his perverseness and sincerity as he tells Winston that he enjoys their conversations.

Much of what Winston recalls in the Ministry of Love occurs when he is either dreaming or drugged. Orwell's descriptions of the Ministry of Love, especially its stark white light, lend a dreamlike, or nightmarish, quality to the events. Even O'Brien's voice has a hypnotic effect, and Winston falls in and out of consciousness, suffering numerous blackouts, which we assume result from the intense pain of his torture.

We are reminded of Julia's statement, "They can't get inside you," as O'Brien continues to batter Winston to rid him of "defective memories." Orwell's description of Winston finally submitting to the Party's control conveys a real sense of the struggle. O'Brien's delight in his role as torturer is apparent in the long dialogue that ends with Winston's shaken belief that "2 + 2 'might equal' 5."

Study Questions

1. What does Winston realize about his continuous beatings?
2. What is the aim of the Party torturers?
3. What becomes Winston's only concern?
4. Who is in charge of Winston's torture?
5. What does O'Brien think is wrong with Winston?
6. What does O'Brien throw down the memory hole?
7. What happens whenever Winston insists that O'Brien is holding up four fingers?
8. What was the Party's purpose in bringing Winston to the Ministry of Love?
9. What does O'Brien predict will happen after Winston's death?
10. According to O'Brien, what is the information Winston will never know?

Answers

1. Winston realizes the beatings are matter-of-course.
2. The torturers aim to humiliate Winston and destroy his power of reason.
3. Winston's aim is to find out what the Party wants him to confess, confess to the crime, and avoid a beating.
4. O'Brien directs the interrogation.
5. O'Brien thinks that Winston suffers from a defective memory.
6. He throws the photo down the memory hole.
7. Winston is subjected to electric shock.
8. Winston has been brought here to be cured.
9. O'Brien predicts that no one will remember Winston, as if he had never existed.
10. Winston will never know if the Brotherhood exists.

Suggested Essay Topics

1. The focus is on O'Brien in these chapters. Explain what Orwell is saying about the power-hungry through him. What character traits does O'Brien possess? Why does he claim to enjoy talking to Winston? Why do you think he allows Winston to question him?

2. Contrast O'Brien's definition of "reality" with that of Winston. What do you think is the foundation of each man's belief?

Part III, Chapter 3

Summary

Having completed the first phase of his treatment, "learning," Winston moves to the second stage, "understanding," which he must complete before being allowed to advance to the third stage, "acceptance."

O'Brien, who admits to collaborating on Goldstein's book, says that because the proletarians will never revolt, the Party will rule forever.

Winston now understands the "how," but O'Brien also tells him "why." Winston believes that O'Brien will tell him that the Party rules for the good of the majority. When he shares this view with O'Brien, he receives another jolt. O'Brien claims that the Party seeks power for its own self-gratification. He illustrates using Nazi Germany and Stalin's Russia as examples of failures that could not admit their real motive: power.

O'Brien continues to explain that the real meaning of power lies in its collective characteristic; individuals can only have power when they give up their individuality. Secondly, power is power over the mind; therefore, external reality is unimportant. Since the Party controls the mind, reality stems from inside the skull.

O'Brien is proud that the Party can accomplish anything by making mankind suffer. In the Party's society, the emotions are hate, fear, triumph, and self-abasement. O'Brien graphically describes a boot stamping on a human face—forever.

The most frightening word to Winston is "forever." Winston maintains this is impossible. He is not sure how, but he is sure that

the Spirit of Man will defeat the Party, for a society based on hatred cannot exist.

O'Brien offers proof that Winston is wrong. First, he plays a recording of the conversation they had had the night of Winston's visit to his apartment when Winston vowed to commit so many outrageous crimes against his fellow man for the Brotherhood. As further proof that the human spirit can be defeated, O'Brien makes Winston strip to his underclothes and look into a mirror.

The skeleton who returns his look is scarred and has an inflamed varicose ulcer. The curvature of the spine is pronounced. Reaching into Winston's mouth to jerk out one of the eleven teeth remaining, O'Brien observes that Winston is literally rotting away.

As Winston collapses in tears, O'Brien points out that escape from the misery is possible at any time he chooses. The only thing left is to betray Julia. Despite the fact that he has confessed to many aspects of their relationship, he still has not denied loving her.

Winston suddenly asks when he will be shot. O'Brien claims he does not know, but that the shooting is a certainty.

Analysis

Orwell satirizes the foundations of totalitarianism through O'Brien's explanation of Party ideology. While departing from the standard interpretation of the motives of any totalitarian state, which is the welfare of its entire body, O'Brien claims that the motive of Oceania's Party is unique in that the Party seeks power for its own benefit. Through life in Oceania, Orwell caricaturizes the idea that there could be any noble-sounding idea behind the control of the masses, for this is a perverse society based on fear and hatred.

The bleak vision of the novel becomes more pronounced as the reader witnesses Winston's physical deterioration. Orwell calls him a "skeletonlike thing" and a "creature" to suggest that the Party has succeeded in stripping him of his humanity. The color "gray," which describes Winston's body, might more traditionally be reserved to detail the deterioration of a corpse. Even though we have always known that Winston's willingness to defy that Party would be punished, O'Brien's description of the "thing" has dramatic impact.

Study Questions

1. Give the three stages of Winston's reintegration.
2. What is O'Brien's opinion of Goldstein's book?
3. Why does the Party seek power?
4. What power is most important?
5. Where does O'Brien believe reality exists?
6. How does the Party exert its power over humans?
7. What is the foundation of the Party's world?
8. What does Winston see when O'Brien forces him to look into the mirror?
9. What is the only degradation that has not yet happened to Winston?
10. What is the only certainty in Winston's life?

Answers

1. The three stages of Winston's reingetration are learning, understanding, and acceptance.
2. O'Brien says Goldstein's book is preposterous.
3. O'Brien says the Party seeks power for its own sake.
4. The most important power is power over the mind.
5. O'Brien believes that reality exists inside the skull.
6. The Party exerts its power by making man suffer.
7. The foundation of the Party's world is hatred.
8. Winston sees a skeleton when he looks in the mirror.
9. Winston has not betrayed Julia.
10. Winston's only certainty is that he will be shot.

Suggested Essay Topics

1. Man's inhumanity to his fellow man is a central element of the theme as the effects of Winston's torture begin to make

themselves known. What does O'Brien tell Winston about the history behind man's suffering? What is the foundation of the Party's philosophy?

2. Describe Winston's physical state. What words and phrases are suggestive of death? Explain why O'Brien seems to take pleasure in Winston's deterioration.

Part III, Chapters 4 and 5

Summary

Since the beatings have stopped, Winston slowly has grown stronger, spending much time thinking and dreaming. Acknowledging how futile it had been to resist the Party's power, Winston recognizes his own insignificance by mechanically writing, "Freedom Is Slavery," and, "Two and Two Make Five." Then, he writes "God is Power." Although he remembers some contrary things, he dismisses the incidents as false memories.

Winston practices "crimestop," a Newspeak term for the automatic process by which the mind stops any dangerous thought. In the back of Winston's mind, however, is the recognition that the only sure thing in his life is the certainty that he will be shot from behind. What remains unclear is when this will occur.

In his cell Winston, who is hallucinating, cries out for Julia, an action he immediately regrets. Thoughts of the bullet return. His cell door opens and in walks O'Brien, who seems disappointed that although Winston has been "cured" intellectually, he still presents a problem because he hates Big Brother. He tells Winston that the final step toward love of Big Brother will occur in Room 101, where the worst thing in the world is located.

The worst thing in the world, as it turns out, is all in the mind. In Winston's case the worst thing in the world is his fear of rats. As Winston begs for mercy, O'Brien slowly approaches with a cage containing enormous, squealing rats.

O'Brien tells Winston that the cage will be placed over his head, and when the rats are released, they will leap onto his face and devour him. Winston now knows that the only way to save himself is to interpose someone else's body between himself and the rats.

Panic sets in as the mask is lowered over his head. Desperate to save himself, Winston betrays Julia.

Analysis

After the beatings stop, Winston spends much of his recovery in a dreamlike state that lends an aura of fantasy to the next developments in the plot. Superficially it seems as if Winston's "cure" is almost complete until he "hallucinates" about Julia and further punishment becomes imminent. Not surprisingly, Winston dismisses the "hallucination" while worrying over the mysterious Room 101.

We have been prepared for Winston's ultimate torture, being devoured by rats, by their earlier intrusion into the room above Charrington's shop and Winston's revulsion. Orwell makes his point that the mind is a shaper of reality through O'Brien's series of graphic images describing the rats: "They leap onto your face and bore straight into it. Sometimes they attack the eyes first. Sometimes they burrow through the cheeks and devour the tongue." He also attacks the savagery of common torture practices through the words of O'Brien, who boasts that these practices were common in Imperialist China.

Study Questions

1. What does Winston write on his slate?

2. What does Winston think of his few remaining contrary flashbacks?

3. Define "crimestop."

4. What is Winston's hallucination?

5. What is Winston's immediate reaction after he cries out for Julia?

6. How must Winston change his feelings toward Big Brother before he can be released?

7. Where does Winston's final torture occur?

8. What is the worst thing in the world for Winston?

9. What does Winston believe is the only way to save himself from his torture?

10. Who is the only person to whom Winston can transfer his punishment?

Answers

1. He writes "Freedom Is Slavery" and "Two and Two Make Five."

2. He thinks these flashbacks are false memories.

3. It is the process of developing a blind spot in the mind whenever a contrary thought occurs.

4. Winston has a hallucination of Julia.

5. Winston wonders how he will be punished.

6. Winston must love Big Brother.

7. The torture occurs in Room 101.

8. The worst thing in the world for Winston is rats.

9. Winston believes he can interpose the body of another person between himself and the rats.

10. Julia is the only person.

Suggested Essay Topics

1. Describe Winston's physical state in comparison to his emotional state. Suggest reasons for his dreams and constant lethargy as he begins his recovery.

2. Room 101 as a symbol of the thing most feared has remained a mystery to this point. What is in Room 101? In what way do the events occurring in Room 101 relate to the concept of the mind as a shaper of reality? What earlier chapter foreshadowed the events that transpire here? Explain.

Part III, Chapter 6

Summary

Finishing another Victory Gin, Winston occupies his usual seat in the Chestnut Tree Cafe where his routine is to sit alone in the corner table, drinking gin as he stares at the chessboard. He has been awaiting news of the war with Eurasia; Oceania had always been at war with Eurasia.

Winston's mind wanders as he continues to drink. Staring at the chess pieces in front of him, he briefly entertains the thought that Eurasia might win the war and the Party's power would be shattered, but the thought quickly fades as he traces "2+2=5" in the dust on the table.

Winston sees Julia after his release. Like him, she has changed. Winston likens her body to the stiffness of a corpse. When they unexpectedly meet in the street, they admit to betraying one another. Winston follows Julia, but the appeal of the Chestnut Tree Cafe is overwhelming because the nonstop supply of gin there is too much to resist.

He remembers a childhood experience when he and his mother had had such a wonderful time laughing as they played Snakes and Ladders by candlelight, but he quickly pushes the image from his mind as a false memory, one of the many he gets.

A horn blast announcing victory interrupts Winston's reverie. Winston reacts by drinking more gin. Thinking of himself, he looks at the ever-present poster of Big Brother and weeps. He knows that it is not long until the bullet eliminates him, but somehow this is no longer worrisome, for Winston loves Big Brother.

Analysis

This chapter dramatically illustrates that the Party *can* get "inside you" as it details the drudgery characterizing Winston's life since his release. The theme of alienation comes to fruition as Winston spends most of his time alone in a corner in an alcoholic stupor. This miserable existence has been foreshadowed earlier through the actions of Syme whose vaporization Winston himself had predicted. Ironically, both he and Winston had shared the trait

leading to downfall: intelligence. We can project that the promised bullet will soon arrive.

As Winston stares into the chessboard, we think of the bigger game that has been played for his sanity. And as he drops the white knight onto the board, we think of Winston who, like the knight, has been destroyed in a similar game. Winston's false memory of the laughter he and his mother had shared as they played a childhood game reinforces the fantasy-like quality that characterizes the entire novel from the moment the clock strikes "thirteen" in Chapter 1.

Several critics have faulted the conclusion with its overwhelming pessimism. The concluding sentence, "He loved Big Brother," carries the message that Winston's struggle against the Party is now over and, perhaps, warns the West of the consequences of acceptance of totalitarian ideas which have been so thoroughly satirized here.

Study Questions

1. What is Winston's new hangout?

2. What news is Winston awaiting?

3. What is Winston's usual routine?

4. What does Julia's body remind Winston of when they unexpectedly meet?

5. What do Winston and Julia admit to each other?

6. Why doesn't Winston follow Julia through the streets?

7. What is Winston's latest false memory?

8. What is the telescreen's announcement?

9. Whose picture hangs in the cafe?

10. Whom does Winston now love?

Answers

1. Winston's new hangout is the Chestnut Tree Cafe.

2. Winston awaits news of the war with Eurasia.

3. Winston sits alone in the corner as he drinks gin and stares at the chessboard.

4. Julia's body reminds Winston of a corpse.

5. Winston and Julia admit to betraying one another.

6. Winston would rather drink gin at the cafe.

7. He remembers the time he played Snakes and Ladders with his mother.

8. The telescreen announces victory.

9. Big Brother's picture hangs there.

10. Winston now loves Big Brother.

Suggested Essays

1. As Winston sits at the Chestnut Tree Cafe sipping his gin, we are reminded of the unfortunate Syme who had been vaporized some time before. Based on previous descriptions of Syme, what most likely will happen to Winston? Evaluate Julia's belief that "They can't get inside you" in light of the conclusion.

2. Cite examples to prove that life goes on as usual in Oceania after Winston's defeat. What does Orwell imply about the fate of others who might try to rebel against the Party?

Appendix

The Principles of Newspeak

Summary

This section defines Newspeak, the official language of Oceania, and sets forth its purpose: to meet the specific needs of Ingsoc, or English Socialism, while making all other methods of thought impossible. When Oldspeak has become obsolete, the last link with the past will have been destroyed.

The vocabulary of Newspeak has been built by inventing new words, eliminating old words, and stripping existing words of their finer shades of meaning. Newspeak, based on English, has three classes of vocabulary words:

1. "A" – words used for everyday life; reserved for simple thoughts, concrete objects, or physical actions

2. "B" – words created for political purposes with the proper mental attitude; all are compound; made up without a plan

3. "C" – supplementary; scientific and technical terms

Analysis

The straightforward manner of the appendix and the elaborate care taken to construct the grammar and vocabulary lend credibility to the existence of Oceania.

Some critics believe that Orwell was pointing out the importance of language as a shaper of thought and the inadvisability of narrowing vocabulary to limit its range. When we consider the nature of the words in the "B" vocabulary, the satirical purpose of the novel becomes more obvious, for words like "honor," "justice," "democracy," and "religion" no longer exist. Instead, a few general words cover these terms, and, as Orwell illustrates throughout the novel, destroy them. Winston's job at the Ministry of Truth makes him an agent of this destruction, just as his attempts to write the illicit diary signify his rebellion against the power of language to destroy thought.

Study Questions

1. What is Newspeak?

2. What is the purpose of Newspeak?

3. When is it expected that Newspeak will become the only language in Oceania?

4. Which dictionary will contain the perfected version of Newspeak?

5. What purpose will be served by cutting down the choice of words in the language?

6. Give the composition of the "A" vocabulary.

7. What is the purpose of the "A" vocabulary?

8. What words make up the "B" vocabulary?

9. What kind of words make up the "C" vocabulary?

10. What is the delay in Newspeak becoming a fully adopted language at the present time?

Answers

1. Newspeak is the official language of Oceania.

2. Newspeak aims to meet the ideological needs of Ingsoc, or English Socialism.

3. Newspeak will probably supersede Oldspeak (Standard English) by 2050.

4. Perfected Newspeak will be found in the eleventh edition of the dictionary.

5. Cutting down the choice of words diminishes the range of thought.

6. The "A" vocabulary consists of words needed for everyday life, words already in existence.

7. The "A" vocabulary aims to express simple thoughts involving concrete objects or physical actions.

8. The "B" vocabulary is comprised of words made up for political purposes.

9. The "C" vocabulary contains scientific and technical terms.

10. The delay revolves around problems translating classic and utilitarian literature.

Suggested Essay Topics

1. Discuss the structure and composition of the "A", "B", and "C" vocabularies. Which vocabulary seems closest to its final stage of development? Which vocabulary has undergone the most change from its Oldspeak structure? Why is the "C" vocabulary termed "supplementary"?

2. Discuss the reasons for the delay in implementing the perfected, finalized version of Newspeak. Why does literature present an especially difficult problem? What problems would people such as Winston Smith have in adapting to this new language?

Sample Analytical Paper Topics

These are topics on which you can write a substantial analytical paper. They are designed to test your understanding of major themes and details from this novel as a whole. Following the topics are outlines you can use as a starting point for writing an analytical paper.

Topic #1

The theme of betrayal is a dominant thread running throughout this novel. Give examples of characters and events that contribute to Winston's final self-betrayal. Make it clear that these examples intensify the novel's overall mood of loneliness and alienation.

Outline

I. Thesis statement: *Orwell explores various kinds of betrayal, including self-betrayal, to heighten the mood of loneliness and alienation in* 1984.

II. Party intolerance of betrayal to its ideology

    A. Indoctrination of children to Party policy

    B. Denouncement

    C. Role of the Thought Police

    D. Extermination

    E. Room 101

III. Individual characters' betrayal of one another

    A. Charrington's betrayal of Winston and Julia

    B. Parsons' betrayal by his children

    C. Ampleforth's betrayal by his work

    D. O'Brien's betrayal of Winston

IV. The hope symbolized by Winston and Julia's love affair

    A. The sanctuary of Charrington's room

    B. The lovers' definition of betrayal

    C. Winston's betrayal of Julia

    D. Julia's admittance to betraying Winston

V. Self-betrayal

    A. Winston's capitulation to the Party

    B. Implications of Winston's defeat

VI. Overall pessimism of the conclusion

Topic #2

Orwell uses the recurrent motif of the dream to reveal background, develop character, and foreshadow key events. Analyze these dreams for their implications.

Outline

I. Thesis statement: *Orwell uses the dream, a recurrent motif, as a mechanism to reveal background, develop character, and foreshadow events.*

II. The Golden Country

    A. Part I, Chapter 2

    B. Part II, Chapter 2

    C. Common symbols and significance

III. The sinking ship

    A. Part I, Chapter 2

    B. Part II, Chapter 7

    C. Interpretation as a key to Winston's mother's disappearance

IV. "The place where there is no darkness"

    A. Introduction of the dream with O'Brien as its speaker

    B. The nightmarish wall of darkness

    C. Literal interpretation of the dream

    D. Significance of the rats

Topic #3

That *1984* is a satire on totalitarian states such as Hitler's Germany and Stalin's Russia and a warning to the West is one of the commonly accepted interpretations of the novel. Prove that this is so by showing that Orwell did create a complete, repressive totalitarian state in Oceania.

Outline

I.   Thesis statement: *Orwell's* 1984 *attacks the totalitarianism of the East while warning the West of its consequences.*

II.   Party ideology

    A. One-party system

    B. Hierarchical structure—Big Brother as leader

    C. Total control of society

    D. Party's motive as explained by O'Brien

III. Monitoring as an effort to eliminate insurrection

    A. Thought Police

    B. Telescreens

    C. Hidden microphones

    D. Passport checks

    E. Vaporization

    F. Room 101

IV. Control of mass communication

    A. Function of the Ministry of Truth

    B. Winston's job at the Ministry of Truth

    C. Ampleforth's function as poet

    D. Syme's work on Newspeak

    E. Constant announcements on telescreen

    F. Party motto—control of the past

V. Examples from History

    A. Stalin's Russia

    B. Hitler's Germany

Topic #4

The paperweight Winston purchases at Charrington's shop takes on several meanings before its final destruction during Winston's arrest. Explain Winston's motive for buying the paperweight as well as its symbolic interpretation as it changes throughout the novel.

Outline

I. Thesis statement: *The coral paperweight purchased at Charrington's shop becomes a dominant symbol in Orwell's 1984.*

II. Purchase of the paperweight

    A. Significance of Charrington's shop as the setting

    B. Winston's motive for its purchase

III. Interpretation as a symbol

    A. Relic of the past

    B. Sanctuary of the room

    C. Beauty of the affair, symbol of hope

    D. Destruction of the paperweight/affair

SECTION SEVEN

Bibliography

Quotations from *1984* are taken from the following edition:

Orwell, George. *1984*. Afterword by Erich Fromm. New York: Signet, 1992.

In addition, Fromm's Afterword was indispensable to this study. The following works were often consulted during the course of this work:

Alldritt, Keith. *The Making of George Orwell*. London: Edward Arnold Ltd., 1969.

Bloom, Harold, ed. *George Orwell: Modern Critical Views*. New York: Chelsea House, 1987.

Crick, Bernard. *George Orwell: A Life*. Boston: Little, Brown & Co., 1980.

Gertrude Clarke Whittall Poetry and Literature Fund. *George Orwell & Nineteen Eighty-Four*. Washington, DC: U.S. Government Printing Office.

Gottlieb, Erika. *The Orwell Conundrum: A Cry of Despair or Faith in the Spirit of Man?* Ottawa: Carleton University Press, 1992.

Hammond, J. R. *A George Orwell Companion—A Guide to the Novels, Documents, and Essays*. New York: St. Martin's Press, 1982.

Howe, Irving, ed. *1984 Revisited: Totalitarianism in Our Century*. New York: Harper and Row, 1993.

Kalechofsky, Roberta. *George Orwell.* New York: Frederick Ungar Publishing Co., 1973.

Myers, Valerie. *George Orwell.* New York: St. Martin's Press, 1991.

Woodcock, George. *The Crystal Spirit: A Study of George Orwell.* Boston: Little, Brown & Co., 1966.

Wykes, David. *A Preface to Orwell.* London & New York: Longman Group, Ltd., 1987.

THE BEST TEST PREPARATION FOR THE

SAT* II:
Subject Test

LITERATURE

6 Full-Length Practice Exams

Based on official exam questions released by the College Board

Detailed explanations to every exam question

Far more comprehensive than any other test preparation book

Includes a COMPREHENSIVE REVIEW COURSE of Chemistry covering all major topics found on the exam

Research & Education Association

* SAT is a registered trademark of the College Entrance Examination Board, which does not endorse this book.

Available at your local bookstore or order directly from us by sending in coupon below.

MAXnotes®
REA's Literature Study Guides

MAXnotes® are student-friendly. They offer a fresh look at masterpieces of literature, presented in a lively and interesting fashion. **MAXnotes®** offer the essentials of what you should know about the work, including outlines, explanations and discussions of the plot, character lists, analyses, and historical context. **MAXnotes®** are designed to help you think independently about literary works by raising various issues and thought-provoking ideas and questions. Written by literary experts who currently teach the subject, **MAXnotes®** enhance your understanding and enjoyment of the work.

Available **MAXnotes®** include the following:

Absalom, Absalom!	Henry IV, Part I	Othello
The Aeneid of Virgil	Henry V	Paradise
Animal Farm	The House on Mango Street	Paradise Lost
Antony and Cleopatra	Huckleberry Finn	A Passage to India
As I Lay Dying	I Know Why the Caged	Plato's Republic
As You Like It	Bird Sings	Portrait of a Lady
The Autobiography of	The Iliad	A Portrait of the Artist
Malcolm X	Invisible Man	as a Young Man
The Awakening	Jane Eyre	Pride and Prejudice
Beloved	Jazz	A Raisin in the Sun
Beowulf	The Joy Luck Club	Richard II
Billy Budd	Jude the Obscure	Romeo and Juliet
The Bluest Eye, A Novel	Julius Caesar	The Scarlet Letter
Brave New World	King Lear	Sir Gawain and the
The Canterbury Tales	Leaves of Grass	Green Knight
The Catcher in the Rye	Les Misérables	Slaughterhouse-Five
The Color Purple	Lord of the Flies	Song of Solomon
The Crucible	Macbeth	The Sound and the Fury
Death in Venice	The Merchant of Venice	The Stranger
Death of a Salesman	Metamorphoses of Ovid	Sula
The Divine Comedy I: Inferno	Metamorphosis	The Sun Also Rises
Dubliners	Middlemarch	A Tale of Two Cities
The Edible Woman	A Midsummer Night's Dream	The Taming of the Shrew
Emma	Moby-Dick	Tar Baby
Euripides' Medea & Electra	Moll Flanders	The Tempest
Frankenstein	Mrs. Dalloway	Tess of the D'Urbervilles
Gone with the Wind	Much Ado About Nothing	Their Eyes Were Watching God
The Grapes of Wrath	Mules and Men	Things Fall Apart
Great Expectations	My Antonia	To Kill a Mockingbird
The Great Gatsby	Native Son	To the Lighthouse
Gulliver's Travels	1984	Twelfth Night
Handmaid's Tale	The Odyssey	Uncle Tom's Cabin
Hamlet	Oedipus Trilogy	Waiting for Godot
Hard Times	Of Mice and Men	Wuthering Heights
Heart of Darkness	On the Road	Guide to Literary Terms

RESEARCH & EDUCATION ASSOCIATION
61 Ethel Road W. • Piscataway, New Jersey 08854
Phone: (732) 819-8880   **website: www.rea.com**

Please send me more information about MAXnotes®.

Name _____

Address _____

City _____ State _____ Zip _____